BUDDHISM for BEGINNERS

The down-to-earth guide to integrating
Buddhist practice into your daily life
& developing inner peace and happiness

D1519561

DHARMA AMANTHI

Table of Content

"Teach this triple truth to all: A generous heart, kind speech, and a life of service and compassion are the things which renew humanity."

Buddha

Chapter 1: History of Buddhism

Essence Of Buddhism

More than 2500 years ago in northwestern India, a man of wisdom named Gautama Buddha founded Buddhism. Gautama was born in an affluent family as a prince in present-day Nepal.

As a child, he had all the luxuries of life. However, when he grew up, he was moved by miseries and sufferings in the world. This was the reason he would feel restless even after having all the comforts of life. So, he decided to give up his luxurious lifestyle and adopt poverty. However, even this didn't give him a sense of fulfilment. So he continued his search for enlightenment and contentment. After several years of struggle and search, he found the truth of *Prati ̄tya-samutpa ̄da* (inter-dependent co-arising) while meditating under a Bodhi tree. From then on, his journey of spirituality and fulfilment began. He spent the rest of his life teaching others about how to accomplish this spiritual state.

Interdependence signifies that all things are influenced by many others. All phenomena, including both physical and mental, have many contributing factors and conditions of causation. When we apply the concept of interdependence in our lives, we achieve an in-depth understanding of the true nature of things. We realize that nothing is independent all on its own and that nothing is entirely self-sufficient. Everything exists due to the events that have also co-arisen.

Buddhism is not a religion but a way of life and the path to enlightenment that is obtained by incorporating morality, meditation and wisdom. Followers of Buddhism don't believe in a supreme god. Instead, they concentrate on gaining enlightenment, spirituality and wisdom. When followers achieve this spiritual state, they are said to have experienced nirvana[1].

Buddhism and Science

Buddhist cosmology is based on the idea that nature and human beings are not mutually contrasting, but are harmoniously interdependent. Thus, within the cosmology of Buddhism, the external world has never been thought to as material existence. One of the most representative descriptions of the Buddhist cosmology appears in the Abhidhaemakosabhasya devised during the fifth century C.E. by Vasuvandhu, affirms that at the foundation of the universe a vast ring of wind floats within empty space. The thickness of the ring is 1,600,000 yojana (one yojana is approximately seven miles) and its circumference is 1059 yojanas. Above the ring of wind there is a ring of water, and on the top of the water ring is a ring of metal. There is a layer of water, an ocean, above the metal ring. At the centre of the ocean is a mountain named Sumeru. The height of the mountain is eighty thousand yojanas. Nine mountain ranges and eight oceans surround mount Sumeru, and the sun and moon circle around it. This is the world of the six realms of transmigration known as samsara.

The world of the six realms of transmigration consists of hell (Naraka)the realm of hungry ghosts (preta), the realm of beasts (tiryand: the realm in which beasts kill each other), the realm of human beings (manusa: although humans are in the state of suffering, they have self-awareness of their state of impermanence and ignorance and are capable of seeking the true living), the realm of titans (asura: deities of anger and fighting), and the realm of heavenly beings (devas). These six realms are all the world of suffering.

Until modern Western scientific theories describing the shape of the Earth and the structure of the solar system were introduced into Buddhist nations like India, China, and Japan, the majority of Buddhists believed that this cosmology actually demonstrated the structure of the universe. However, Buddhist cosmology was not created as a chart of the Earth discovered through a geographic survey or astronomical observation. Instead, Buddhist cosmology was a vision created spiritually by Indian Buddhist monks, both Theravada and Mahayana, who meditated upon the towering Himalayan Mountains in the north of the subcontinent. The purpose of this cosmological vision is to unfold the reality of this world, which is filled with defilements and sufferings as living beings transmigrate through the six realms of existence.

Buddhists meditate upon the concept of transmigration of the six realms of existence to awaken to truths of impermanence and vanity and to achieve the state of enlightenment, which is beyond the realms of ignorance. Even today, this spiritual cosmology of Buddhism remains respected within Buddhist communities throughout Southeast and East Asia[2].

Buddhism in India

During the third century B.C.E., King Asoka of the Mauryan Empire, after reflecting on the cruelty and evil of war, converted to the teaching of the Buddha, which taught compassion and peace. Based on Buddhism's egalitarian view of the original nature of all human beings, the king protected all religious traditions equally. He built hospitals for humans and animals, grew medicinal herbs, planted trees on the streets, and dug wells and ponds for the well-being of the people.

At the beginning of the second century C.E., during the reign of King Kaniska of the Kusana Empire, the royal physician Caraka, an ethicist and a Buddhist, compiled a great book on medicine. According to the book Caraka-Samhita: The Collected Medical Treatments of Charaka, human beings must strive to seek three goals: to respect all lives, to obtain fulfilled lives, and to attain the happiness of enlightenment. In India, the practice of medicine was not an independent area of science but was treated as an integrated part of Buddhism, philosophy, and ethics[3].

Buddhism in China and South East Asia

Numerous Mahayana and Theravada Buddhist scriptures dealing with the cure of general illnesses, eye disorders, and dental problems appear from about the late fourth-century c.e. when advances in medicine and pharmacology were made. In Tibet, China, and South East Asia, the study of medicine and pharmacology was based on traditional Indian ayurvedic medicine. Additionally, in China, Buddhists incorporated existing conventional medical practices, including acupuncture, moxibustion (moxa-herb combustion treatment), and medicinal herbs to cure illnesses[4].

Buddhism in Korea and Japan

Many Buddhist monks from the Korean peninsula travelled to India and China to pursue real Buddhism. Others went to Japan to spread and create the foundations of Buddhism in this neighbouring country. These monks significantly contributed to the creation of Japanese culture. For example, Huici, a Korean monk from Koguryo, went to Japan in 595 C.E. and was hired as the tutor of Prince Shotoku. In 602, the monk Guanle from Pekche introduced the studies of astronomy, geography, calendar making, and mathematics. In 610, Tanzheng, a Korean monk from Koguryo presented the Chinese technologies and arts of painting, paper making, and ink production. These technologies were also transferred to nations to the west as Chinese and Korean monks travelled to propagate Buddhism.

In Japan, Prince Shotoku, who studied the Buddhism and politics of the Chinese Sui Dynasty, is recognized for introducing new Chinese architectural technology and encouraging the arts of paper and ink making during the seventh century. He constructed Buddhist temples for the sake of world peace and social equality. In the eighth century the Empress Komyo, influenced by the compassionate spirit of the Tang Dynasty, built the Hidden-in, a house of compassion with social welfare facilities providing shelters for the poor, sick, and orphaned, and the Seyaku-in, a house of medicine with its own medicinal herb garden and pharmacy offering free care and medicine for the poor. The world's oldest printed materials were Buddhist scriptures found in Korea and Japan. These include Hyakumantou-darani, Buddhist scriptures enshrined in three-story wooden stupas, which were made to pay tribute to the war dead in 764.

In Japan, physician-monks appear as early as the seventh century. Although these monks carried the title zenji (meditation master), they were not advanced zazen practitioners but medical caregivers for emperors and aristocrats. The work of physician-monks included the techniques of acupuncture and moxibustion, the creation of medicinal compounds, surgery, internal medicine, paediatrics, ophthalmology, and obstetrics.

From the seventh to twelfth centuries, monks from China, such as Ganjin, and Japanese monks who had studied in China, such as Saicho and Kukai, continued to introduce medical practices, including new medications and breathing exercises. Records indicate that monks in the Nara area—like Kiogan of Todaiji, Kikogan of Toshodaiji, and Ho-shintan of Saidaiji—produced and marketed medicine to support the temple economy. During the thirteenth century, the Tendai School on Mount Hiei established a department of medicine within the monastic complex. From the sixteenth century, Jodo Shinshu temples, in particular, encouraged the production of medicine by famous medical practitioners and donated medicine for the sick.

During the 1920s, work-oriented Morita therapy was developed within Japanese psychiatric medicine. Based on the teachings of Zen Buddhism, especially the concept of nonattachment, Morita therapy teaches that the more one tries to eliminate suffering, the more suffering becomes fixed in one's consciousness. Morita therapy involves giving up the attachment to grief by living with suffering while doing physical work, nurturing the mind, and searching for a new and meaningful way to live. Morita therapy clearly contrasts with modern medical practices, which objectify illness as an enemy to be forcefully conquered[5].

Buddhism in Tibet

Tibetan Buddhism practice includes natural science, medicine, and pharmacology. Tibetan medicine is highly holistic. It focuses on the integrated mind and body and their harmony with the entire universe. *Gyu-shi* (four medical texts) written in the eighth century is one of the world's oldest documents on psychiatry.

At a Tibetan Buddhist hospital located in a four-story modern building in downtown Lhasa, doctors who have also studied modern western medicine treat patients according to traditional Tibetan Buddhist medical practice. They consult charts of human anatomy showing the paths of respiratory tracts, arteries, and chi; charts of pressure points in the human body; and charts of plants and animals used for food. Buddhist doctors in Lhasa also use charts explaining how to diagnose illness by analyzing urine and blood, and they refer to tanka paintings of astronomical charts. This combination of charts represents the fundamental Tibetan Buddhist concept of the interrelatedness of the human body and the universe. This hospital is also attempting to compile a scientific analysis of the psychology of Buddhist enlightenment through modern psychology[6].

"By learning to trust your intuitions miracles seem to happen. Intuitive thoughts are a gift from the higher self."

Susan Jeffers

Chapter 2:
The Values of Buddhism

The main idea of Buddhism is to liberate people from earthly sufferings and adversities. However, that doesn't mean that they will not encounter trials and hardships. It simply means that people will become so enlightened and spiritually aware that their inner selves are at peace no matter what the situation is.

The core teachings of Buddhism are:

1. The Three Universal Truths
2. The Four Noble Truths
3. The Noble Eightfold Path

The Three Universal Truths

1. **Everything is impermanent and changing.** It means nothing lasts forever, be it happiness or trial. Therefore, the best strategy is to stay patient during the course of adversity and humble during the times of contentment.

2. **Impermanence leads to suffering, making life imperfect.** It implies that change is constant, and it can lead to suffering if we don't accept the continuously changing nature of life. Suffering is caused by the discrepancy between impermanence and the desire for permanence. It is the desire for perfection that causes suffering, so by understanding and accepting impermanence, one can be free from suffering.

3. **The self is not personal and unchanging.** It means that the self is just an illusion. If one aims to reach a state of Enlightenment, one must release notions of the "self" and become selfless[7].

The Four Noble Truths

The Buddha's Four Noble Truths are focused on human suffering. They may be described as:

1. **Dukkha.** Suffering is real, and life is all about suffering. Suffering has many causes such as loss, disease, adversity, failure, and the impermanence of pleasure.

2. **Samudaya.** There is always a cause of suffering. Suffering is mainly due to attachment. When we desire to have and control things, it leads to suffering. It can take many forms such as the desire for fame, the desire to avoid unpleasant situations, like fear, anger or jealousy.

3. **Nirodha.** No matter how difficult your situation is. There is al-

ways an end to suffering. You can overcome your attachment by accepting the realities of your life. Suffering ceases with the final liberation of Nirvana (Nibbana). The mind experiences complete freedom, liberation and non-attachment. It lets go of any desire or craving.

4. **Magga.** In order to end suffering, you must follow the Eightfold Path. There is a path for accomplishing this[8].

The Eightfold Path

The Eightfold Path consists of eight ways of behaving, and each way has to be followed because they depend on each other. They relate to wisdom, morality and meditation.

1. **Right seeing and understanding.** E.g. understanding the Noble Truths

2. **Right thought or intention.** E.g. acting considerately.

3. **Right speech.** E.g. avoiding lies, gossip and controversial speech. Speaking the truth.

4. **Right action.** E.g. integrity and not hurting any living being.

5. **Right work or livelihood.** E.g. avoiding unlawful jobs and works.

6. **Right effort.** E.g. making efforts to overcome desire, selfishness and attachment.

7. **Right mindfulness.** E.g. practising meditation and adopting spirituality.

8. **Right concentration.** E.g. freeing the mind of distractions before meditation[9].

Karma

Karma is a Sanskrit word that means action. In Buddhism, karma has a more specific meaning, which is a voluntary or wilful action. Whatever we say, do or think set karma into motion. The law of karma is, therefore, a law of cause and effect as defined in Buddhism. It means that each action a person takes will affect them at some time in the future. This rule also applies to a person's thoughts and words, and the actions other people take under that individual's instructions. A good deed will lead to a future beneficial effect, while an evil act will lead to a future harmful effect[10].

Cyle of Rebirth

Another essential doctrine of Buddhism is the cycle of rebirth. According to Buddhists, our lives are cycles of death and resurrection called samsara. When a person dies, their energy passes into another form. And according to the principle of karma, the person who performs good deeds and actions will get a better life after rebirth. Similarly, evil actions of a person will result in a hard life after their rebirth.

Chapter 3: Tibetan Buddhism

Tibetan Buddhism is a branch of Buddhism that blends the learnings of the *Mahayana* Buddhism, the Tantric and Shamanic, and an ancient Tibetan faith called Bon. Although Tibetan Buddhism is often compared to the Vajrayana Buddhism, this branch of Buddhism has a few crucial changes. Today, Tibetan Buddhism is a religion that is in exile. It was forced out of its homeland in Tibet when the nation was conquered by the Chinese. Buddhism was so ingrained within the Tibetan people that it was believed one in every six Tibetan men was a Buddhist monk.

The face of Tibetan Buddhism is the Dalai Lama, who have resided in exile since fleeing the Chinese occupation in 1959.

History

Towards the 8th Century, Buddhism was a major presence in the life of Tibetan people. It originated from India and came to Tibet by the insistence of the Tibetan kind, Trisong Detsen, who asked two Buddhist teachers to come to Tibet and translate Buddhist texts into Tibetan. The first of these two monks, named Shantarakshita, built the very first monastery in Tibet. His successor, Padmasambhava, came to Tibet to use his wisdom to resolve spiritual disturbances in the monastery.

Tibetan Buddhism Groups

The groups that formed within Tibetan Buddhism are as follows:

Nyingmapa. This group was founded by Padmasambhava and is the oldest sect of Tibetan Buddhism. It is used in the West because of its teachings in the Tibetan Book of the Dead.

Kagyupa. The Kagyupa group was founded by a Buddhist named Tilopa, and its important instructors include Naropa, Milarepa, and Marpa. The head of the Kagyupa tradition was the Karmapa Lama.

Sakyupa. This group was formed by Gonchok Gyelpo and his son.

Gelugpa. The Gelugpa is known as the Virtuous School and was created by Tsong Khapa Lobsang Drakpa. It is this traditional group that it headed by the Dalai Lama.

New Kadampa Tradition. The New Kadampa Tradition is another major Buddhist school founded by a Tibetan named Geshe Kelsang Gyatso. Several Buddhists claim that this tradition falls outside the regular Buddhism.

Features of Tibetan Buddhism

Tibetan Buddhism has certain special features, such as:

- The status of the Dalai Lama (teacher)
- Concern for the relationship between life and death
- Certain rituals and initiations

- Detailed visual symbolism
- Some elements of previous Tibetan faiths
- Mantras

Meditation

Tibetan Buddhism is big on rituals and other spiritual practices, including mantas and yogic practices. This branch of Buddhism also gives importance to supernatural beings like gods and spirits. This metaphysical ideology integrated in Tibetan Buddhism has allowed it to develop artistic traditions, like paintings and statures. Other graphics are used to understand Tibetan Buddhism's relationship with metaphysical godlike figures and deities in society.

Visual aids are actually incredibly important to the Tibetan Buddhists. They use pictures and structures in their public prayers, including wheels and flags. They claim that it provides a reminder of the spirituality present in the physical domain.

Lay people and monastic communities both practice Tibetan Buddhism. The lay version of Tibetan Buddhism emphasizes on outwardly religious practices like rituals at temples and pilgrimage. Their focus on inner spirituality is much less than in other schools of Buddhism. Their pilgrimage includes prostrations and repeated prayers using prayer wheels and flags. Tibetan Buddhism has several festivals, and they treat their funerals with importance as well. Lay Buddhists offer physical support to monasteries, and in turn the monks organise their rituals.

Aspects of Tibetan Buddhism

Lama. In Buddhism, teachers are referred to as lamas. These are senior members of monastic communities, such as monks and nuns, but can be lay people and married people as well. Lamas always usually reincarnations of previous lamas. These senior instructors are learning in

Buddhist philosophical teachings and sacred texts, as well as the skills of ritual.

Dalai Lama. The word 'Dalai' is a Mongol term that refers to the ocean. The Dalai Lama is called this as his wisdom represents the depth of the ocean. The first Dalai Lama who received this title was Sonam Gyatso. He was the 3rd Dalai Lama, as the previous ones received this title posthumously. The current Dalai Lama is the 14th Dalai Lama, Tenzin Gyatso.

Tantra. Tantra influences much of Tibetan Buddhism. This branch of Buddhism borrows several elements from Tantra, such as complex rituals and techniques. Although Tanta originated in India, it appears in both Hindu and Buddhist traditions. Tantra brings elements of magic and heavenly beings into Tibetan Buddhism. Spiritual techniques like mantras, mandalas, and ceremonies are incorporates from Tantra to this branch of Buddhism.

Rituals. Simple rituals and spiritual practices are common in Tibetan Buddhism, such as making offerings to statues of Buddha and attending public teachings and ceremonies. Tibetan ceremonies usually take place in temples and are quite loud and bright. These visually appealing festivals feature brass instruments, cymbals, and gongs. Formally dressed monks chant musicals. These can take place in monasteries, as well.

Other Practices. Numerous advanced rituals and practices are an important part of Tibetan Buddhism. Most of them can only be performed by those who have reached a higher level of spiritual understanding and power. It is only possible for those who have sophisticated knowledge of Tibetan Buddhism. Some of these practices include spiritual ones which require tough meditations and elaborate visualisations. Senior Tibetan Buddhists and Lamas have attained much greater control over their body and spirit than other human beings. They are said to be able to control their body temperatures, heart rates, and other anatomical functions. This is why it is only in their power to perform these advanced practices.

Life and Death. Another important aspect of Tibetan Buddhism which is highly emphasized upon is the awareness of death and our own impermanence. Everything around us is constantly dying, including our own cells and the plants and living beings around us. Everything is reminding us of our impermanence on this planet.

This reminder is not meant to sadden us or cause us despair, nor does it mean that we should impulsively start running after each of our desires. Instead, it simply means that our stay on this earth is a gift. Every moment is a present, and we should live in it. Buddhists try to see the value of the present moment of existence during their meditation and other religious practices.

Being aware of the impermanence of life allows one to have a greater understanding of their minds. We come to realize, with the teachings of Tibetan Buddhism, that only spiritual items have any lasting power. All material things that have physical form die. That is their ultimate fate.

On the topic of life and death, we will talk about how Tibetan Buddhism requires us to prepare for death adequately and with proper measures. Practitioners of this holy branch of Buddhism use meditation and other exercises to visualise death and thus prepare for bardo, the stage between life and rebirth. Working towards an understanding and acceptance of the permanence of death is an inevitable part of any Tibetan Buddhist's journey.

Some other ways that Buddhists from this school of Buddhism prepare for death is by participating in helping those who have already passed away. It is said that this aids the dead, along with allowing the practitioners to learn what the experience of bardo entails, before they enter it. Even if you cannot gain enough spiritual awareness to understand bardo from helping out the dead, you will still gain a deeper insight into life by accepting its transience.

Bardo. As previously mentioned above, bardo is the state between the life and rebirth of a Tibetan Buddhist. All groups of Tibetan Buddhism have a different understanding of what bardo truly is. It is considered as a state that lasts for forty-nine days.

How a person experiences bardo is said to depend on their spiritual understanding in this life. A person who is trained about bardo and its trials may find them easy to overcome. To an untrained person, bardo might be a confusing state. Their negative attachments to materialistic things and people may cause their rebirth to be not as positive as it could have been.

Traditional Tibetan Buddhists believe that in bardo, dead people are helped in passing through by a Tibetan Buddhist teacher or lama. They read prayers and perform various religious rituals and practices from a book known as the Book of the Dead, which allows the dead people to break free of worldly attachments. Some sects of Buddhism believe that lamas have the power to lift the consciousness of the dead person from their body, in order to prepare them for rebirth.

Tibetan Buddhism instructs that it is the job of the people left behind to help the dead pass through on their journey. To do so, spiritual work is required that is believed to grow the virtues of the deceased, ultimately helping them achieve a better rebirth.

Several Tibetan Buddhists also insist that those who are pass away can, during the 49 days of bardo, look clearly inside the minds of those who are still alive. This enables the living people to help their deceased relatives and ancestors by meditating, clearing their minds of impure and evil thoughts, and engaging in spiritual rituals.

The New Kadampa Tradition

Although the New Kadampa Tradition is said to fall outside the mainstream teachings of Tibetan Buddhism, it is one of the most popular schools of Buddhism in the United Kingdom. It is a fast-growing religion that follows the teachings of the original Mahayana Buddhism. It has over 900 centres of meditation spread across 37 countries. The founder of the New Kadampa Tradition was a Tibetan meditation teacher called Geshe Kelsang Gyatso.

New Kadampa Tradition practitioners state that this school of Tibetan Buddhism allows one to learn Buddha's traditions and his method of meditation, as well as provides an alternative way of life that promotes serenity, peace, and living in harmony with other beings.

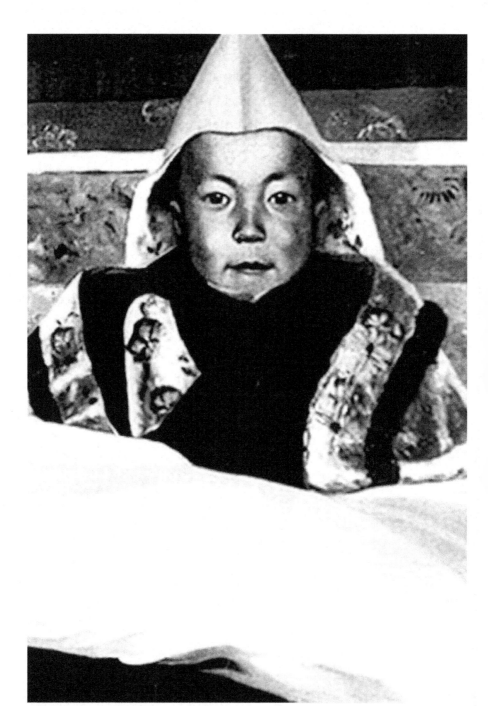
Dalai Lama when was a boy.

Chapter 4:
The Dalai Lama

We previously briefly touched upon the Dalai Lama in the previous chapters, and now you will learn about them in more detail. If you had heard of Buddhism before reading this book, chances are that you have also heard of the Dalai Lama. In Tibetan Buddhist circles, the Dalai Lama is the head monk who had assumed the responsibility of governing Tibet until the Chinese took over in 1959. The concept of the Dalai Lama is a tradition belonging to the Gelugpa group, which is an important sect of Tibetan Buddhism.

There have been only fourteen Dalai Lamas to date. As mentioned before, the first two Dalai Lamas got their titles after their deaths. Buddhists believe that the current Dalai Lama is a reincarnation of a past Dalai Lama who was reborn to finish their earlier incomplete work. Instead of moving on from the wheel of life, the Dalai Lama has contiued on living to complete their important work on this Earth.

Buddhists refer to a person who decides to be continually reborn as *tulku*. The first *tulku* is said to be the reincarnation of Gedun Drub. The second, Buddhists believe, is Gendun Gyatso. The name 'Dalai Lama' literally means 'Ocean of Wisdom'. It was not conferred until the third reincarnation, who was Sonam Gyatso in the year 1578.

Currently, Tenzin Gyatso is the present Dalai Lama.

How the Dalai Lama is Chosen

When the present Dalai Lama passes away, it is the responsibility and job of the High Lamas of the Gelugpa sect and the Tibetan government officials to find his reincarnation. This is usually a boy who was given birth to around the same time as the passing of the Dalai Lama. It can take a few years to identify the new Dalai Lama. For the current Dalai Lama, it took four years to find him. There are many ways to find out who the next Dalai Lama is. Some of them are:

Dreams. It is possible that one or more of the Higher Lamas may dream about a mark or place where the new Dalai Lama can be found.

Smoke. As the previous Dalai Lama is cremated, the High Lamas will look for signs in the smoke, like its direction, and search accordingly.

Holy Lake. High Lamas may also go to a holy lake called Lhamo Lhatso or Oracle Lake in central Tibet and watch for signs there. Some experience visions or an indication of direction. The home of Tenzin Gyatso, the current Dalai Lama, was also determined from this lake.

Once the Dalai Lama's location has been determined, the High Lamas go to his home with a series of gifts and artefacts. They present the boy with the artefacts. Of these artefacts, one or more of the items belong to the previous Dalai Lama. If the boy chooses the artefacts that belong to the previous Dalai Lama, it is seen as a sign that he is the reincarnation of the Dalai Lama.

However, this procedure is not unchangeable. If the majority of the population of Tibet insists that the method to find the Dalai Lama is changed, it may be changed and another may be used. The Dalai Lama's search is limited to Tibet only usually, although third Dalai Lama was born in Mongolia. The current Dalai Lama insists that his reincarnation will be in an imprisoned nation, that is, not in any country run by China.

Dalai Lamas are manifestations of the patron saint of Tibet and are thought of as holy beings in schools of Tibetan Buddhism. Born in 1935, the current Dalai Lama is said to be the reincarnation of Thubten Gyatso. His Holiness Tenzin Gyatso, was born to a peasant family in Amdo, a province in north-eastern Tibet. His village was known as Takster. Although the High Lamas, senior teachers of the Gelugpa tradition, had been on the search for the reincarnation of the previous Dalai Lama for many years, several signs finally pointed to this young boy, Lhamo Thondup, as the real one.

It is said that the face of the 13TH Dalai Lama turned to the north-east direction after was embalmed. Along with this, one of the High Lamas had a vision when they went to search for signs in the sacred Oracle Lake. All these signs pointed to the village Amdo as the place where the High Lamas would find the next Dalai Lama, and ultimately that is where they found him.

The vision of the High Lamas also directed towards a three-storied monastery that supported a gold and turquoise coloured roof. Additionally, they also envisioned a house with a peculiar drainage system. In a place called Kumbum in Amdo, a monastery fit the description of the vision that the High Lamas had had. After a thorough and detailed search of the villages in the neighbouring regions, the house of the current Dalai Lama, Lhamo Thondup, was finally discovered. The young Dalai Lama was only three years old at that time.

A party consisting of officials and the High Lamas formally went to Lhamo's household and presented him with a few items. This is the final test taken to ensure that the child certainly is, without a doubt, the next Dalai Lama. Lhamo was asked to choose between certain items, which included the belongings of the deceased Dalai Lama: a rosary and a bell. It is said that young Lhamo immediately picked up the possessions of the previous Dalai Lama, claiming them to be his.

Then, young Lhamo, at the age of five, was admitted at a local monastery, where he completed his training. He was taught by the highest ranking monks in all of Lhasa, which is the capital city of Tibet and his residence at that time. In 1950, when Lhamo turned fifteen years of age, he was officially crowned. He continued his studies until the age of twenty-five, achieving high honours. Lhamo was officially renamed Jamphel Ngawang Lobsang Yeshe Tenzin Gyatso. He gained control and governance of Tibet, although on all maps of the world, it was only a province in China.

When China underwent political evolution in 1950, their government planned to gain control of Tibet officially. This was unfeasible and not a popularly-liked idea by people of Tibet, and they began a protest in 1959 that demanded an end to the control of the Chinese nation. Thousands were killed in the political unrest that followed, and the revolt was swiftly crushed by the Chinese. The Dalai Lama, fearing for his life, sought refuge in India where the Indian Prime Minister of the time, Jawaharlal Nehru, welcomed him with open arms. Thousands of his supporters and followers were also taken in by India.

With the Prime Minister's permission, the Dalai Lama formed the Tibetan Government in Exile in a place called Dharamsala in India. A society was created that adhered to the Tibetan Buddhist culture and language, and followed its arts and religion. This society was promoted by the Dalai Lama and his followers.

The 14th Dalai Lama, Tenzin Gyatso, is the first Dalai Lama to travel to the West. His charming manner drew in support for Buddhism from all corners of the world, as well as for the movement for Tibetan resistance. In the year 1989, the Dalai Lama was presented with the Nobel Peace Prize for maintaining non-violent policies with the Chinese government and keeping his supporters at peace, despite knowing that they would be much happier to take up armed resistance.

The Nobel Peace Prize's Committee stated:

"The Committee wants to emphasize the fact that the Dalai Lama in his struggle for the liberation of Tibet consistently has opposed the use of violence. He has instead advocated peaceful solutions based upon tolerance and mutual respect in order to preserve the historical and cultural heritage of his people."

In the past few years, several universities have presented peace awards to the Dalai Lama as well as honorary doctorate degrees because of his efforts towards peace and extraordinary writings of Buddhist philosophy. His remarkable leadership skills have also been commended by leaders worldwide and his ability to maintain peace and freedom remains unparalleled.

In 2011, the Dalai Lama gave up his role as the political leader of Tibet, insisting that the leader should be one who is freely elected by the will of the people. He had previously announced his semi-retirement in 2008 after a gallstone surgery. All around the world, the Dalai Lama is a well-known name and face. He has participated in speaking events and awed the people of the world with his charismatic demeanour. Today, the eighty-year old spiritual leader remains just as influential and revered around the globe as ever.

"If there is any religion that could respond to the needs of modern science, it would be Buddhism."

Albert Einstein

Chapter 5:
Buddhism in the
21st Century

21st century is the century if technology and inventions. Science has provided the world with countless amenities for comfort and pleasure. Nevertheless, we observe that people are distressed and miserable. As the luxuries of life are advancing, depression, anxiety, and mental illnesses are also increasing. People are anxious because they don't feel a sense of security. Many psychological studies have revealed that satisfaction and security are related to our minds. If we don't have peace of mind, no amount of money or luxury can please us. Safety can refer to freedom from physical danger. When our minds are convinced that we are safe from physical danger, we feel happy and content.

On the contrary, when our mind can sense a possible danger, we end up becoming upset and worried. So, we concluded that mind is the most significant thing in one's life. Psychology, as the science of mind and academic discipline, was introduced in the 19th century. However, Gautama Buddha founded Buddhism about 2500 years ago. He taught us all those things related to human mind thousands of years ago that psychology is discovering today. Buddha said, "Mind is the forerunner, and mental states are mind-made."

According to the teachings of the Buddha, man is the component of five aggregates, namely: form, feeling, perception, volition, and consciousness. Out of these five, the only form is physical, and the other four are mental. These mental aptitudes are very important in contemplating man. As science is predominant in the world today, scientists can take a new step for the advancement of science through recognition of ethical and religious dimension. The Dharma taught by the Buddha is not something outside the world and beyond experience. Therefore, it wouldn't be wrong to say that Buddhism and science go hand in hand. The Dharma realised by the Buddha is a discovery of the existing phenomena in the Universe. It is, therefore, a universal and everlasting truth about the Universe.

Science today has already acknowledged that certain teachings of the Dhamma are correct without any doubt. However, it took a long time for science to come to this conclusion. Similarly, it will take a long time to obtain scientific proof of other aspects of Buddhism too. However, if we research it on our own, we will find many amazing truths that prove that Buddhism is the most science-friendly religion that doesn't rely on fictional stories. This is the reason that Buddhism is the fourth largest religion in the world. It is estimated that around 488 million people in the world – that makes 9 to 10 per cent of the world population – practice Buddhism. As more people are becoming aware of the philosophy of Buddha, the number of followers of Buddhism is increasing [11].

Buddhism and Modern Science

First of all, Buddhism favours the idea that if we want to prove something, we must talk about it based on empirical evidence. If there is a contradiction between what we analyse—either directly or through reasoning based on perception—and what Buddhist scriptures say, then we have all right to reject the scriptures and stick with what we have identified empirically. To put it simply, the evidence of our own reasoning and finding has to be the touchstone.

Tibetan tradition often cites a quote of Gautama Buddha:

"Just as a goldsmith tests to see whether something is gold by touching it to a touchstone, by rubbing it, by heating it, so too, oh monks, you should accept my words only after examining them and not out of respect for me."

Of course, scripture is valuable. However, it is not what we can never deny. In the context of Buddhism, what humans actually need is experience. By experience, it means something that can positively transform our personalities. Only intellectual understanding is not enough. No matter how many of the Buddha's dissertations we read, it will never be equivalent to our own experience. So, right from its beginning, Buddhism has an inherent sense that while the Buddha's teachings are obligatory to steer us to correct the path, at a certain point, we need to leave that behind to go with our own direct experience.

Another way in which Buddhism can be referred to as a science-friendly religion is how it engages in a very comprehensive assessment of the mind. Within the Abhidharma, one of the three forms of canonical Buddhist literature, there's a great deal of explanation about the mind itself and various ways of analysing how it works. It asks: How do attention and perception work? If I am attached, how is attachment operating? How does it make me behave? How do I counteract attachment? How do I learn to recognise attachment? The numerous ways of examining the mind that we find in the Abhidharma literature are quite in-depth and detailed. Many scientists who are seeking some alternative perspectives on the workings of the mind are quite intrigued by this literature.

One of the significant features of these Buddhist accounts of the mind is that they do not presume that there is a sole controller or ego that is governing all of these processes. That belief has turned out to be a generally acknowledged position among neuroscientists, who have not recognised a part of the brain that controls everything else. There's no evidence of any single controller within the various brain processes that constitute consciousness. So, Buddhism's strong account of the workings of the mind along with the position that declines the idea of a single controller is another way in which Buddhism is significantly in agreement with modern mind sciences.

When you evaluate all these facts, you can infer that there is a likelihood for a good dialogue with science and also that in a certain way, Buddhism is scientific. However, Buddhism holds a broad set of ideas that need time to be acknowledged as compatible with science. Therefore, promoting Buddhism to a dubious public by playing up its apparent agreements with science, is not a good idea. I have come across some Buddhists who try to do this, and it's quite disappointing. This encourages the notion that Buddhism needs to be validated by science to be "true," which is not at all the case. We must remember that Buddhism does not require validation by science. In fact, it is science that requires validation by Buddhism. After all, the great Gautama Buddha achieved enlightenment without knowledge of any scientific theories.

Though the disciplines of science and Buddhism work on completely distinct standards that touch each other only slightly, there's no reason science and Buddhism can't peacefully co-exist and even, sometimes, illuminate each other. Buddhism continues to offer a behavioural path forward, one that apparently adapts to each new time and culture while technically not changing at all.

Zen teacher John Daido Loori said:

"When science goes deeper than the superficial qualities -- and these days science does go much deeper -- it remains constrained to a study of the aggregates. From tree morphology -- trunk, bark, branches, leaves, fruit, seeds -- we dip into tree chemistry, then tree physics; from molecules of cellulose to atoms, electrons, protons. When the true eye functions, it goes beyond looking and enters the realm of seeing. Looking speaks to what things are. Seeing reveals what else things are, the hidden aspect of reality, the reality of a rock, a tree, a mountain, a dog or a person."

"Set your heart on doing good. Do it over and over again, and you will be filled with joy."

Buddha

Chapter 6: How Your Thoughts Impact Your Life

Have you ever thought what makes humans more special than all other living beings?

It's our ability to think about and process our feelings. We, humans, are made up of several emotions, negative and positive. We express these emotions according to the situations prevailing in our lives. Sometimes we feel happy. At other, we feel stressed. One thing that I have noticed and perhaps you may also feel that these days people undergo negative emotions and feelings more than positive ones. As the world is advancing and the luxuries are becoming a part of our lives, stress and anxiety are also increasing manifold. The suicide rate is also growing, and sometimes everything seems to be in chaos. Why is that so? With all these technological advancements and inventions, we are supposed to be happier and more peaceful, but we are not. The reason is, our actions are being driven by our thoughts.

If you ever talk to your parents or grandparents, they will tell you how happy and content they were during their youth. They didn't have the internet. They didn't have smartphones. They didn't have many other luxuries. Still, they were joyous. Do you know why? Because there was no competition. People lived their lives for themselves and not for others. They were grateful for what they had. Over the past few decades, especially with the evolution of social media, things have entirely changed. People have gone crazy to show the happier part of their lives to people on the internet. There is a never-ending competition going on. Our lives have become artificial. Our happiness, achievements, talents and so forth have got associated with likes and comments.

We seek the validation and approval of our friends and the people around us in everything we do. Even at parties, family dinner or any other social gathering, for the most part, people are busy capturing their selfies and uploading them on social media. We have forgotten the true meaning of fun and joy. In such a situation, when we see someone happier than ourselves, we develop an inferiority complex. We get carried away by emotions of ungratefulness, self-pity and distress. And this is where the destruction starts. Our thoughts, good and bad, have a significant impact on our health. I often say that our health is the by-product of our thoughts and emotions.

We will discuss it later as to how our thoughts impact our health and lives, later in this chapter. First, I want you to know how our feelings, thoughts and behaviour work and how they are linked.

How Our Thoughts, Feelings and Emotions are Connected

As I said above that one of the major reasons of anxiety and stress is that we don't have control over our thoughts. In fact, we can't even identify our feelings, let alone control. Sometimes, we feel upset for no reason, right? We feel overwhelmed, but we can't seem to figure out the cause. And we end up concluding that there is no reason of our sadness. However, that's not true. There is always a reason, but sometimes we are not able to identify that. In psychology, therapists often use Cognitive Behavioural Therapy (CBT) to treat the patients of depression, anxiety and other mental illnesses. This is a talk-therapy, in which the therapist asks several questions to the patient. This therapy is based on the idea that our thoughts, feelings and behaviours are interconnected. First of all, a thought develops in our minds. This thought leads to a particular feeling, and then the feeling drives our behaviour. We keep behaving according to our thoughts and feelings until we identify that specific thought and learn to control it. The objective of this therapy is to help the patients identify their thoughts.

Understanding your thoughts is the first step to control your behaviour. Let's discern it with the help of an example. Just suppose that you are feeling upset and down. As a result of this feeling, you ignored all your work and kept lying in your bed throughout the day. You don't want to talk to anyone, and you just believe that you are feeling upset without any reason. Due to this feeling, you have a terrible headache. You want to get rid of this feeling and relax, but you can't because you don't know where this feeling came from. How will you deal with this situation?

Here comes the solution. You just need a piece of paper and a pen or pencil. Take a moment and think about the last time, you felt happy on a particular day. Your mind is just like a storeroom. When you try to think about your last happy moment, a series of flashbacks will run in your mind. It may take some time, but you will certainly find your last happy moment. Now, start pondering over the event that led you to think negative. If you are single, perhaps you saw a picture of a happy couple on your Facebook. Or if you are financially struggling, maybe you came across a vlog of your friend who is now making a fortune through these videos. It can be anything, but after seeing that, unconsciously a thought sprang to your mind that you are worthless or no one likes you. With this thought, a feeling of sadness and dejection appeared in your mind, and it led you to ignore your work and responsibilities and behave in a certain way, such as lying in your bed or fighting with a family member or friend.

Many times, your bad behaviour is due to you being unaware of your thoughts. When you are able to recognise your thoughts, you are able to control them before ending up with malicious behaviour. Our thoughts and feelings greatly influence our lives, especially our health. Therefore, it is necessary to take control over them before the damage becomes unmanageable.

How Our Thoughts Affect Our Physical and Mental Health

Being emotionally strong and stable does not imply that you should be happy all the time. It only means that you are aware of your feelings and can handle them, whether they are positive or negative. Emotionally healthy people also experience stress, rage, and grief. However, they know how to manage their negative feelings. Before diving into the details of these approaches, let's first understand what negative and positive emotions are.

Positive Emotions

I know most of you must be aware of the difference between negative and positive emotions. Still, I am describing them briefly here just to draw your attention to something which is based on a false idea. Positive emotions are those emotions that we feel pleasurable to experience. Some of the most common positive emotions are:

- Love
- Joy
- Satisfaction
- Contentment
- Interest
- Amusement
- Happiness
- Serenity

Negative Emotions

Negative emotions are the emotions that we find unpleasurable or don't like to experience. They make us feel uncomfortable, and we always want to get rid of them. Some of the common negative emotions are:

- Fear
- Anger
- Disgust
- Sadness
- Rage
- Loneliness
- Melancholy
- Annoyance

If you search on the internet, you will find many articles that share with you the techniques to eliminate negative emotions from your life forever. Sounds quite idealistic and fascinating, doesn't it? However, I find this idea vague and impractical. For example, anger is a negative emotion, and if someone close to you does anything wrong, it is natural to get angry. Similarly, the demise of a loved one will undoubtedly make you sad. Then how is it possible to remove negative emotions from your life? In facts, negative emotions make us feel the joy of positive us. If negative feelings didn't exist, life would become monotonous. The idea of cognitive therapies or Buddhist teachings is not to remove negative emotions or thoughts from your life, but it is to channelise them. The purpose of understanding your thoughts is to be able to steer them in the correct direction. If your feelings and thoughts make you argue with your loved ones and you find it disturbing and dangerous for your relationship, you need to learn how to land in a healthy conversation instead of arguing and fighting.

Negative feelings become unhealthy when they are prolonged and begin to interfere with your daily life. Extended periods of negative emotions like anxiety, sadness, and hopelessness can create chronic stress, which disturbs the body's hormonal balance, reduces the number of brain chemicals required for happiness, and damages the immune system. Science has identified that chronic stress can actually decrease our lifespan. Similarly, poorly managed or suppressed anger can also lead to several physical and mental health conditions, such as:

- High blood pressure
- Cardiovascular diseases
- Digestive disorders
- Infection
- Headache
- Fatigue

- Insomnia
- Anxiety
- Depression
- Social withdrawal
- Severe changes in metabolism (i.e. overeating or under-eating)

Isn't it unjustified to ourselves to develop such issues when we have the power to avoid them? Maddy Malhotra is an international motivational speaker, coach and author. One of her thoughts immensely inspired me. She put down, "Depression, anger, and sadness are states of mind, and so are happiness, peace, and contentment. You can choose to be in any of these states because it's your mind."

I know it's easier said than done. However, channelising your thoughts is not an impossible task. Thankfully, we have the teachings of Buddha to guide us. In the previous chapter, I mentioned that many things that psychology and science are discovering today had been brought to light by Buddha thousands of years ago. One of the first insights of Buddhist meditation practice is to identify that our minds have a mind of their own. It might seem that our thoughts are downright outside of our control, and we have no choice about the kinds of things that drift across our minds. Does it mean, we are simply at the mercy of a mind, out of control? For most of us, most of the time, the answer is yes. But the teachings of the Buddha tell us it need not be this way.

The Vitakkasanthana Sutta is a discourse contained within the Pali Canon (a collection of scriptures) of Theravada Buddhism. In this Sutta, the Buddha describes five approaches to overcome negative thoughts.

Five Approaches of Vitakkasanthana Sutta

Now let's get back to the five approaches of The Vitakkasanthana Sutta. Buddha has used the example of a carpenter in this Sutta to describe the techniques of overcoming negative thoughts and feelings. However, I will explain it in easier words so that you can grasp the gist of this concept readily.

First Approach

According to Buddha, when you have identified a problematic thought in your mind, the first approach is replacement. Replace that unwholesome thought with a wholesome one. For example, if the fear of failure is disturbing you, try to supplant that feeling by thinking that you will try to find ways to overcome failure. At first, the technique of replacement may seem complicated and artificial. However, with practice, you become habitual and only require the slightest expenditure of mental energy.

Second Approach

Buddha says that if you think that the first approach is not working for you, you should try the second approach that is the reflection on results. Think about the repercussions of your unwholesome thoughts. Identify the damages these unskilful thoughts will cause to your relationship, career and health. Once you are aware of the consequences, you may become able to calm your emotions down.

Third Approach

If you feel that even the second approach is also not making any difference, you can switch to the third approach, which is redirecting. According to this technique, at the time of anger, distress and anxiety, one should try to shift their attention to something else. For example, if you had a fight with your spouse and you are feeling overwhelmed, instead of prolonging the argument of thinking about it, just redirect your attention to something else. You may watch a movie, read a book or talk to a friend. After some time, when your anger subsides, you will be in a better position to think about the situation wisely.

Fourth Approach

If you feel that all three approaches are not benefiting you, you may try the fourth approach, which is reconstructing the formation of an unwholesome thought. With this technique, you think about the events that led to the creation of specific thoughts and feelings. By systematically reconstructing the formation of an unwholesome thought, you are able to return it to its leading causes and see how it is rooted in a false apprehension of reality.

Fifth Approach

The fifth and the last technique for overcoming distracting thoughts is resisting the "evil mind" through the "good mind." The Buddha advises that one should clench their teeth and press their tongue against the roof of their mouth as if they are beating down, constraining, and crushing the evil mind with a good mind. This approach might appear a rather impractical way of relaxing thinking patterns. But the intensity of this method is instructive if taken in the proper spirit.

Did you realise how important our thoughts are for transforming our lives? If you incorporate the teachings of Buddhism in your life, you will be amazed by the dramatic changes it brings to your life. In the next chapter, we will understand how being aware of our thoughts, bodies, minds, and our surroundings can transform our lives.

"Mindfulness is a way of befriending ourselves and our experience."

Jon Kabat-Zinn

Chapter 7: Mindfulness and Buddhism

You may have heard or read the word mindfulness if you search for the ways of reducing stress and anxiety on the internet. However, not many of us really try to incorporate it into our lives because it seems complicated and time-consuming. Before diving into the details of how mindfulness and Buddhism connect, lets first understand what mindfulness is.

What is Mindfulness?

In today's busy world, most of the time, we are multitasking. While working on an important assignment, you also keep an eye on your phone not to miss any important messages. Similarly, homemaker women have to watch out for their kids while cooking or while folding laundry. Even on weekends, we are busy trying to accomplish necessary tasks. In all this hustle and bustle, we lose our connection with the present moment without even realising. We perform our daily tasks like a robot without even focusing on them. We don't try to know how we feel while doing a specific job. And hence, gradually, we become entirely detached with our thoughts and feelings. In this situation, our thoughts get in the driving seat of our lives' vehicles and then our actions and behaviours are driven by our thoughts and chaos begins.

To regain the connection with our thoughts and present moments, experts suggest that we must learn to focus on and live in the present moment. And here comes mindfulness for our help. Mindfulness is the practice of deliberately focusing your attention on the present moment. It is about being aware of our thoughts and accepting them without being judgmental.

Benefits of Mindfulness

Practising mindfulness has proved to be one of the best ways to bring positive changes in health, attitudes and behaviours.

Following are a few benefits of mindfulness:

Mindfulness Improves Well-Being

Incorporating mindfulness to your life may support many attitudes that contribute to a happy life. Being mindful makes it easier to enjoy the pleasures in life as they occur. It helps you fully indulge in activities, and develops resilience to deal with adverse events.

When people include mindfulness in their daily routine, they realise that they are less likely to get carried by worrying thoughts about their future or regrets over the past. When they focus on the present moment, they learn to enjoy the moment that they are focusing on instead of being occupied with concerns about success and failure. Moreover, they are able to develop deep connections with others.

Mindfulness Improves Physical Health

In addition to improving well-being, it is discovered that mindfulness practices help improve your physical health in a variety of ways. Mindfulness can fasten your recovery from cardiac diseases. It can help you: keep your blood pressure normal, reduce chronic pain, improve sleeping patterns and relieve digestive disorders.

Mindfulness Improves Mental Health

If you have ever been to a psychologist for some therapy, you might have an idea that psychotherapists consider mindfulness meditation as an essential element in the treatment of various mental conditions such as depression, substance abuse, eating disorders, relationship conflicts, anxiety and obsessive-compulsive disorder.

These are just a few benefits of integrating mindfulness techniques in your daily life. You will experience hundreds of them when you start practising it yourself.

Mindfulness and Buddhism

Though the concept of mindfulness has become internationally widespread in the past decade, its roots reach 2,500 years into the past. Over the centuries, mindfulness practices have taken different forms, but their purpose has always remained the same, that is to end suffering. In the late 1970s, Dr Jon Kabat-Zinn, a professor of medicine emeritus at the University of Massachusetts, developed an eight-week stress-reduction program called Mindfulness-Based Stress Reduction (MBSR). The purpose of this program was to lower stress and enhance well-being. The effectiveness of this program was supported by thousands of scientific research studies. Since then, it became quite popular, and a variety of mindfulness therapies, mindfulness coaching and mindfulness exercises were introduced. Mindfulness practices are often taught without following any particular religion, but their roots connect to the early teachings of the Buddha.

Even Dr Jon Kabat-Zinn disclosed that his MBSR program is based on a type of Buddhist meditation called Vipassana. in fact, the idea to come up with such a program sprang to his mind while he was meditating. The word Vipassana comes from the ancient Pali language of India and is often translated to English as "clear awareness" or "insight".

So, the essence of mindfulness is based directly on the historical teachings of the Buddha who presumably used the technique to achieve nirvana, i.e., a deep insight resulting in the end of suffering. According to the teachings of Buddha, mindfulness is one of two key qualities that are developed when doing vipassana meditation. The other quality is concentration.

The ancient text known as the Satipatthana Sutta; translated into English as The Discourse on the Establishing of Mindfulness makes it evident that it was the Buddha who laid out the first-ever set of mindfulness instructions, known as the four domains of mindfulness.

Four Domains of Mindfulness

Mindfulness of the Body

Mindfulness of the body refers to recognising each part and function of the body individually. Some ways to experience mindfulness of the body include:

- Being mindful of the breath
- Being mindful of walking, sitting, lying down and standing

Being aware of the thirty-two part of the body, i.e. hair of the head, hair of the body, nails, teeth, skin, flesh, sinews, bones, marrow, kidneys, heart, liver, membranes, spleen, lungs, bowels, intestines, gorge, dung, bile, phlegm, pus, blood, sweat, fat, tears, grease, snot, spittle, oil-of-the-joints, urine and brain.

Clear comprehension of the purpose, suitability and reality of this domain[12].

Mindfulness of Feelings

The second domain is the mindfulness of feelings. It signifies being aware of the feelings such as

- Pleasant, unpleasant or neutral
- Worldly and spiritual
- Arising, disappearing and manifesting[13]

Mindfulness of Mind

The third domain is mindfulness of the mind. This implies understanding the quality of the mind and developing awareness of the background. It includes contemplating whether your mind

- Is greedy or not?
- Contains hatred or not?
- Is with or without delusion?
- Is contracted or expanded?
- Is developed or not?
- Is freed or bound?
- Is concentrated or scattered[14]?

Mindfulness of Dhamma

According to Henepola Gunaratana's book The Four Foundations of Mindfulness in Plain English, the elements of the fourth domain of mindfulness include:

1. **The Five Mental Hindrances.** Sense-desire, anger, sloth-and-torpor, worry and flurry, sceptical doubt.

2. **The Five Aggregates of Clinging.** Form, feeling, perception, men-

tal-formations and consciousness

3. **The Six External and Six Internal Senses.** Eye and form, ear and sound, nose and odour, tongue and flavour, body and touch and mind and idea.

4. **The Seven factors of Enlightenment.** Investigation of Dhammas, energy, rapture (joy), mindfulness, tranquillity, concentration and equanimity.

   The first three are to be developed when the mind is dull; the last three, when the mind is agitated. Mindfulness is to be developed in all circumstances.

5. **The Four Noble Truths** (explained in chapter 2)[15]

Techniques of Mindfulness

We talked a lot about how mindfulness will bring some amazing changes to your life and where it originates from. I am sure you must be thinking, "how can I incorporate mindfulness in my life?"

So here, I am sharing a few ways briefly that you can adopt to become mindful.

Meditation

The words meditation and mindfulness are often used interchangeably because it is one of the best ways to be mindful. Many people misunderstand meditation believing that it is a way to vacate your mind from worrying thoughts and emotions. However, this is not true. No one can vacuum their head of thoughts. The idea of meditation is to suspend judgment and unleash our natural curiosity about the workings of the mind, approaching our experience with warmth and kindness, to ourselves and others.

A Simple Meditation Practice

Meditation mainly focuses on the breath because the physical sensation of breathing is always there, and you can use it as an anchor to the present moment.

- Find a place that is quiet and peaceful and sit comfortably. You can sit on a mat, cushion, couch, chair or anything that you feel comfortable in.

- Cross your legs in front of you. If on a chair, rest the bottoms of your feet on the floor.

- Straighten your upper body but don't stiffen. Your spine has natural curvature. Let it be there.

- Place your upper arms parallel to your upper body. Rest the palms of your hands on your legs wherever it feels most natural.

- Drop your chin a little and let your gaze fall gently downward. It's not necessary to close your eyes. You can simply let what appears before your eyes be there without focusing on it.

- Start feeling your breath. Bring your attention to the physical sensation of breathing: the air moving through your nose or mouth, the rising and falling of your belly, or your chest.

- During practice, your attention will leave the breath and wander to other places. Don't worry; that's pretty okay. There's no need to block or eliminate thinking. When you notice your mind wandering, gently return your attention to the breath.

- Don't be too hard on yourself. Instead of grappling with your thoughts, practise observing them without reacting. Just sit and pay attention. Come back to your breath over and over again, without judgment or expectation[16].

- When you feel you are done, softly lift your gaze (if your eyes are closed, open them). Take a moment and notice any sounds in the environment. Notice how your body feels right now. Notice your thoughts and emotions.

- Practice it every day religiously and gradually you will start noticing a change in your thought process. Obviously, meditation is not magic. However, if practised regularly, it will bring about many dramatic changes to your life.

Yoga

Another amazing technique of practising is mindfulness is yoga. Many people believe that yoga is all about losing weight and toning your body. Well, this is one of the benefits of practising yoga, but the main essence of yoga is to help you achieve a higher level of connection and awareness between the mind, body, and spirit. Just like meditation, yoga also aims to build a deeper connection to and understanding of the self. If you have ever practised yoga or even read about it, you may know that yoga also teaches you to tune into your breath and pay attention to bodily sensations. In fact, one of the basic poses of yoga that is Easy pose (Sukhasana) done the same way as meditation. You just sit comfortably, close your eyes and focus on your breath. This simple pose, if practised regularly, does wonder to your physical and mental health. There are several postures of yoga that will help you become mindful. Some of them include Mountain Pose, Tree Pose, Low Lunge, Reclining Bound Angle Pose, Triangle Pose and so forth.

Prayer

Whether you are a follower of Buddhism or any other religion, prayer is something that is associated with hope and aspiration. It is a spiritual connection with a high power that includes gratitude, adoration and surrender. When you start praying, you demonstrate gratitude to the divine source, and it automatically makes you feel aligned. It generates positive emotions in your mind, and you feel relaxed. Through prayer, you connect to your divine source and present all your worries and distressing thoughts in front of that particular source. For a few moments, you detach from the outside world and focus only on your problems and their solution. Prayer is a way to admit that there is something more substantial than the self and to allow that divine source to relieve the pressures of day to day living.

If you feel that above mentioned methods are time-taking and you are not able to take out that much time from your busy schedule, you don't need to worry. There is still hope for you. In the next chapter, I will share some techniques that you can incorporate while driving or while even while working on your laptop. You can always transform yourself if you have the will to do so.

"All that we are is the result of what we have thought. The mind is everything. What we think we become."

Buddha

Chapter 8: How to Integrate Buddhism in Your Life

Following Buddhism means incorporating peaceful spirituality-based traditions in your life. Our spiritual health needs constant nourishment. It is important to implement certain specific techniques that allow you to detangle the knots within your spirituality with ease. Buddhist practices can fit easily within even the busiest of lifestyles. In fact, integrating Buddhism into your life will even allow you to follow your faith and religious practices with more tranquillity and spirituality. Most Buddhist practices are aimed at making your lifestyle more serene and meaningful. They urge you to reflect upon yourself and your present surroundings. Practicing mindfulness and introspection are some easy ways to integrate Buddhism within your daily practices.

Mindful Breathing at Any Time of the Day

Mindful breathing is a simple enough technique that builds a strong resistance to stress, anxiety, and anger, within oneself. There are many numerous benefits of implementing mindful breathing into your daily routine. Some of these are:

- Lower heart rate and blood pressure
- Reduce depression
- Reduce burnout and fatigue
- Manage chronic body pain

The act of mindful breathing consists of being actively aware of your inhaling and exhaling. In order to be completely mindful of your breathing, you have to take note of your breathing patterns and allow yourself to become more relaxed and at peace. Focus on the air entering your mouth and nostrils and how smoothly it exits. Feel your lungs expand with fresh air and then return to normal. When you learn how to do this without distractions, you will have mastered the art of mindful breathing.

Some of the steps you can take to practice mindful breathing are:

1. Sit in a comfortable and relaxed position, with your feet on the ground.

2. Take note of your breathing patterns. Allow yourself to feel your mouth, nose, and lungs as you go through the emotions of breathing.

3. Allow your mind to wander, but make sure that you ground yourself after a certain amount of time has passed.

4. Remain seated for five to eight minutes in silence. Keep taking notice of your inhaling and exhaling movements. Feel the air enter your lungs and leave.

5. After a few moments have passed, stand up and offer gratitude and appreciation for the day.

Mindfulness Shower

Taking a mindfulness shower is the perfect way to start your day. Waking up and mentally preparing yourself for a long day of work or school can be an arduous task. It's only when you jump in the shower that you are briefly away from the hustle and bustle of your busy life. A mindfulness shower is the perfect opportunity to observe and take note of your surroundings and present moment. The time you spend in the shower allows you to be in touch with your body. Practicing mindfulness during the shower means that you can connect your spirituality and feelings to your physical form easily.

Some ways to implement mindfulness during your daily shower are as follows.

1. Place all your electronics outside the bathroom, or far enough to not disturb you as you shower. Distractions from your phone can disrupt your mental processes.

2. Place your towel and freshly-pressed clothes in a clean place, where you can wear them immediately after drying of. As you undress, name each article of clothing you take off and place it down with utmost care and attention.

3. Think about how you are going to cleanse your mind and body in the moments going forward.

4. As you stand under the shower, allow your body to feel the water as it hits your skin.

5. If your thoughts start to wander, make a mental note of it. Allow your mind to explore, but not to dwell on the past or worry about the future.

6. Change the order in which you wash your body. Alter the pattern in which you clean your body every time you shower.

7. The time duration of your shower isn't important. You can take either a quick shower or a longer one.

8. Dry yourself when you are finished with the shower.

9. Step outside and wear your clean clothes.

Ten Minutes Morning Routine

It is quite hard to bring yourself to a focused state-of-mind immediately after waking up. Getting up can prove to be a challenge, especially if you usually run late for office or school. In our hectic lifestyles, mornings are usually incredibly busy. All you notice is a flurry of activity where you grab a breakfast sandwich, take two sips of coffee, and head on over to your car or bus.

A ten-minute morning routine will help bring you to the right mindset and explore the different possibilities of the day in front of you. If you start your day with this routine, it will not only maximize your productivity and effectiveness, you will also be filled with positive vibes to take on the day ahead. Locking a morning routine is extremely reliant on your willpower. If you can manage to hold it, it can enhance and improve your life in countless ways!

Begin every day with the best possible attitude with a small ten-minute routine. Take the following steps to make the most of it.

1. Hydrate yourself.

2. Breathe deeply for one to two minutes.

3. Stretch your body. Allow yourself to feel active and awake.

4. Practice gratitude. You can do this by giving thanks or maintaining a gratitude journal.

5. Visualize the day ahead of you. Envision the success that is in the palm of your hands.

Quick Five Sense Mediation

The goal of the Five Sense Meditation is to bring calmness and peace to ourselves using our five senses. Humans are sensual beings. Our senses ground us to our surroundings. The Five Sense meditation routine allows us to meditate using the sense. Its steps are detailed below:

1. **Sight**

Look around you and count five things that you can see. Try to pick things that you wouldn't normally notice.

2. **Touch**

Take note of four things in your surroundings that you can touch. Imagine what they would feel like and their texture is.

3. **Hearing**

Look around you and try to notice three things that you can hear. Focus on the background sounds. These can be birds chirping or an electronic appliance ringing. It can be anything.

4. **Smell**

Focus on two things that you can smell. These can include the food cooking in the kitchen or candles burning in your room.

5. **Taste**

Finally, focus on one thing that you can taste. Take a sip of cool water, or bite into a piece of chocolate. Notice the current flavor in your mouth.

The Five Senses Meditation will help ground you and make you feel more like a part of your surroundings than you did before. It allows you to be fully aware of your environment and the things present in it.

Ten-Minute Office Yoga at Your Desk

A ten-minute routine of office yoga can alleviate a lot of stress that you have accumulated over the course of the day. Practicing yoga at your desk can be the solution to a lot of your problems. If you experience chronic lower back pain, a stiff neck, or sore shoulders from working in the office for hours on end, a ten-minute office yoga routine can be just the thing you need. Some of the poses you can practice are:

Seated Cat Cow Pose

The Seated Cat Cow Pose is a simple yet powerful yoga pose that won't take you more than three minutes. All you have to do is place your hands on your thighs and inhale. While inhaling, arch your back and tighten your shoulder blades by squeezing them together. Finally, exhale and place your chin on your chest.

Allow your breathing to guide your movement and move back and forth for one minute. Follow a gentle rhythm aligned with your inhalation.

Seated Spinal Twist

The Seated Spinal Twist allows you to work your muscles while sitting down. Twist your body to the right while breathing in and out and grasp the back of your chair to stabilize yourself. Hold your position for fifteen seconds. Then do the same with the left side.

Another variation of this yoga posture involves placing your arm behind your back and easing into the twist. The Seated Spinal Twist only takes one minute to complete, leaving you fully refreshed after.

Mountain Pose

The goal of this traditional yoga pose is to get your blood flowing. Sitting in an office for a very long time lets your muscles become inactive and slow. You start getting tired and sleepy. The best way to combat those feelings is to perform this five-minute yoga pose.

This office yoga technique involves standing up with your arms kept at your sides, palms front. Tighten your thigh muscles while allowing your belly to remain soft and stay in this position for a total of sixty seconds. Keep your breathing slow and steady to gain the maximum benefits of this yoga pose.

Neck Stretches

Neck stretches are great for relieving tension that is pent-up in your neck. While working on a desk, we often have to lower our neck to look down and that builds the tension up. To start this fairly simple and easy desk yoga pose, tilt your head to your chest and use your hand to increase the stress on it by easing it forward. Stay in this position for ten seconds, and then bring your head to right. Increase the stretching by keeping your left hand on your head. Hold this position for ten seconds, and then repeat with the left side.

These neck stretches can also be done by rotating your head to each side and holding for a few seconds. Finally, bring your head to the back to let go of the tension in the front of your body. This series of neck stretches targets the different muscles in your neck and shouldn't take more than a minute to complete.

Shoulder Stretches

Shoulder stretches are stretches that are aimed at the muscles in your shoulders and upper back. These can help open up your chest, too. Shoulder stretches involve tensing your muscles, and then releasing them. This allows you to feel relaxed and active. These stretches relieve stress, as well.

Modified Downward Dog Pose

This version of the Downward Dog pose focuses on several different areas of your body. It allows you to stretch your calves, shoulders, and hamstrings. In this yoga pose, you need to stand a short distance away from the desk and raise your arms over your head. Bend forward until you touch your desk. This yoga pose provides maximum freshness when performed for one minute.

Seated Figure 4 Stretch

The Seated Figure 4 Stretch targets your hips and relieves back pain. In this pose, you must sit straight and keep your right ankle on top of your left knee. Gently push down on your right knee. Stay in this position for thirty seconds and vary the pressure on your knee. Now repeat with your other ankle and knee. Hold your left ankle over your right knee for thirty seconds. Perform this pose for three minutes to experience the stretch fully.

Wall Sit

The Wall Sit is an easy enough yoga pose. This refreshing activity challenges your lower body. To perform the Wall Sit pose, you must stand with your back flat against a wall and gently slide down into a sitting position, keeping your thighs parallel to the floor. Stay in this position for sixty seconds. It might be difficult to stay for even that long, but don't give up. This strengthens your thighs and works on your lower body's muscles. Slowly stand up and walk back to your desk.

Chair Pose

The Chair Pose works your lower body and spine. This is a challenging yoga pose that may seem simple at first, but don't be fooled. The Chair Pose is performed next to a wall. You begin in the Mountain Pose until you build your strength and then you lower your body until your thighs are parallel to the floor. Hold this pose for thirty seconds and then slowly rise to a standing position.

Seated Relaxation Pose

The Seated Relaxation Pose is an excellent way to end your office yoga routine. It allows you to feel relaxed at the end of the session. In this yogic pose, you start by sitting down on your chair with your spine straightened. Bring your hands to your thighs and close your eyes. Inhale deeply and allow yourself to exhale. Hold each breath briefly within your lungs. Focus on your breathing and try not to dwell on the work you have to get back to. After a few moments have passed, whenever you are ready, open your eyes and take in the world around you. Take a few seconds to review your yoga routine and then return to your job. If you have time, you can take a short break to meditate, as well.

"The whole secret of existence is to have no fear."

Buddha

Chapter 9: Zen Habits to Bring Peace in Your Life

Have you ever met someone who seems to be completely at peace with themselves and everything around them? Even if their surroundings are dipped in chaos, these people will emanate a certain kind of tranquility. People like these are connected to their spiritual selves through practices like meditation and yoga.

One approach to bring peace and calmness within our lives is to implement Zen habits. Making Zen habits a part of your daily routine will help you escape the stress and anxieties of your day. Our lives can be chaotic and overwhelming. Practicing Zen habits throughout the day can definitely alleviate some of those.

What is Zen Buddhism?

You might be wondering what Zen Buddhism actually is. The word 'Zen' is the Japanese pronunciation of a Chinese word that means "meditation". Originating in the 8th Century, Zen practices have since been popular all around the world, especially in the West.

Zen Buddhism emphasizes on an individual's personal experience. It is a practice-oriented tradition that focuses on meditation. Zen training centres implement practices like 'Zazen' (or the Sitting Zen) where monks and Zen practitioners rise early in the morning to meditate and participate in long silent retreats.

To become a student of Zen Buddhism, you must devote your life to ongoing practice, kindness, and the search of serenity. Zen Buddhism urges its students to find long-forgotten and deeply buried answers to their quests, namely, the meaning of existence and purpose of your birth. Zen Buddhism helps you face the challenges in life by allowing you to be more open towards your feelings and emotions. Once you embark on the path to Zen Buddhism, you will come to embrace that good and bad are a part of life, and that your existence and ultimate death are a gift. This is the essence of Zen Buddhism.

Some of the teachings of Zen Buddhism are as follows:

- Whatever happens, happens at the right time.

- Home is where your thoughts are peaceful.

- It is better to laugh at a mistake than to spend time regretting it.

- Unhappiness will enter through doors left open.

- If your words don't improve a situation, stay silent.

- If you are tempted to give up, know that victory is near.

- Someone who points out your flaws is not necessarily your enemy. Someone who might speak of your virtues is not necessarily your friend.

- Live patiently and wait for the rewards to come.

Seven Zen Habits to Bring Peace in Your Life

Implementing Zen habits will allow you to face the difficulties in life with vigor and calm. Zen teachings instruct us to be patient and attentive to our surroundings at every moment. We are to concentrate on the here and now. Some of the main life-changing Zen habits are:

1. Breathe

Your breath is the connection between your mind and body. You might have noticed your breathing become rapid when you are faced with danger. This is because your state-of-mind and breathing rate are connected.

Breathing is incredibly important and is an essential part of trying to remain calm in the face of chaos. Having control over our breathing allows us to quickly pacify our mental states when faced with risk. In order to integrate this Zen teaching into your daily routine, make a habit of taking seven deep, focused, and deliberate breaths once or twice a day. Once you find out the benefits of this remarkable habit, you will find yourself practicing it more and more.

2. Tell a New Story

In order to be whoever you want to be, you have to tell yourself a new story. Telling yourself a new story means to affirm your wants and needs in the way you choose. In order to make a habit stick, it is essential to tell yourself to do it. You must affirm new things to yourself daily. If you are prone to being short-tempered, tell yourself that you will be patient and kind. Some of these sayings can include:

"I am calm and peaceful."
"I spread love to all who I meet."
"I am brave and powerful beyond imagination."
"I am resilient in the face of adversity."

Affirming and reaffirming these sayings over the course of a day will surely allow you to feel the changes in your attitude and personality yourself within a matter of days.

3. Smile

Sometimes, even just smiling can end up making us happy. It is true that there is a certain kind of contagious joy in smiles. Just looking at someone smile can cause vast orchids of happiness to bloom inside our chests. This Zen habit is certainly a popular one.

The act of smiling allows your brain to release neuropeptides that directly reduce stress levels. Peaceful chemicals and mood stabilizers like dopamine and serotonin are released too, with a simple smile. Your heart rate and blood pressure tend to relax. Smiling has an incredible mood-boosting effect on your whole body.

Take a few moments of your day to feel happy and smile. Simply turning the corners of your mouth can release feelings of joy and happiness inside you.

4. Reprogram your perception of suffering

Suffering is a state of mind. It is said that suffering is the discomfort you feel as you grow stronger and take on fiercer hurdles in life. As the name suggests, this Zen habit instructs us to change our way of perceiving what suffering really is. When we take on rigorous physical challenges, we consider the burning of our muscles as suffering. As time goes on, the burning fades and is replaced by a feeling of strength and power. It is the same with our thoughts and feelings. When we feel ready to give up, that is when we are the closest to victory. Zen teachings state that when we are uncomfortable, we are growing. Think of your pain as a teacher instead of a problem. Allow yourself to learn from it.

5. Go into nature

Our day-to-day lives consist of being faced with electronics like phones and computers. The best way to escape the hustle and bustle of today's modern world and its distractions, is to head out into nature.

Disconnect from your phones and laptops, and take a hike. Or simply go for a picnic with someone you love. You may listen to soothing tunes as you sit on comfortable grassy lands on top of a hill. Allow yourself to be one with the nature. Open your hart to the beauty of your surroundings and allow them to bring peace to you.

6. Be present

Being present is as simple as the name suggests. At any given moment, be fully aware of your surroundings and allow yourself to immerse in them completely. Look around. Take note of the ongoing world. Make sure you don't miss the moment by being too distracted or dwelling on the past.

7. Meditate

Meditation allows you to nourish your spiritual and emotional health. It is a catharsis of sorts, where you release negative energy into the world and adopt positive vibes. Practicing meditation also allows you to form a deeper connection to yourself, ultimately resulting in great inner peace. There are many ways to meditate, including practicing mindfulness and yogic activities. Meditation is a simple technique that allows you to get to know yourself better and bring more peace into your life.

Chapter 10: A Deep Dive into Zen Buddhism

We already learned a little about Zen Buddhism in the previous chapters, but now let us take a deep div into this particular school of Buddhism.

The Birth of Zen

The word Zen originates from the Chinese word '*ch'an*' which literally means absorption. After the word travelled east to Japan in the 8TH century, it became 'Zen'. Zen is a part of the Buddhist school, *Mahayana*, which started in China, crossed over to Vietnam, and headed to Korea, before finally settling in Japan.

After the birth of Buddhism in India, many sects and sub-sects came into being. These sects carried several scriptures, and the scriptures in turn contained numerous commentaries. After spreading through the Central Asian route, Buddhism entered China. The Chinese adhered to the teachings of Confucius and Tao, and so they opposed any ideology from other Asian regions who they called the 'Middle Kingdom'. The understanding of Buddhism was difficult as the script had to be translated from Sanskrit to Chinese, which was deemed next to impossible. The mixing of cultures, Indian and Chinese, led to the restructuring of Buddhism. This evolution of Buddhism eventually led to the creation of Zen. Zen became an entirely new sect of the Buddhist religion and became the most successful school by far in the Tiger countries.

The Evolution of Ch'an to Zen

Zen, which was *Ch'an* at that time, was received enthusiastically in Japan. The Samurai class, who were warriors with strong political powers, used to practice Zen throughout their life. The Chinese immigrants who introduced Zen to Japan were greatly educated people. They introduced things like Chinese literature, calligraphy, philosophy, ink paintings, as well as religious practices to their Japanese students. These students, who developed an interest for Zen Buddhism, then travelled to China to learn more about this new mind-opening meditation.

The ink monochrome paintings that we have today are a type of art form closely related to Zen paintings. Zen Buddhist monks were the first artists to paint in this quick manner, trying to express their religious beliefs, as well as personal views in their art. The subjects of these paintings were their patriarchs, their teachers, and their enlightened leaders. However, with time the paintings changed their subjects to more secular themes. These included paintings of bamboos and orchids, as well as birds which were associated with scholarly symbolism in China. The paintings then evolved and changed to be about literary figures and landscapes. We can tell that they changed into more general things, rather than personal feelings. There is more on Zen Art in the next chapters.

Attributes of Zen Buddhism

Zen, which is simply meditation-based Buddhism, has little to do with traditional Buddhism's doctrines, laws, and regulations. Zen has neither scripture nor rituals, and is passed on from Zen Buddhist monks to their disciples, often through hard and difficult training. Although Zen is a part of Buddhism, changes have been made and improvised over the years passing through generations.

Zen is inscribed in informal, slang Chinese language, using the lessons of Taoism, Confucianism, and various poetries. The Buddha himself is rarely mentioned as the literature is based upon legendary short stories of great monks and masters.

Zen emphasizes greatly on the simplicity and importance of living naturally; a style that is expressed by the terms *wabi* and *sabi*. These concepts express a sense of loneliness, naturalness, and coming of age. In short, this means that a misshapen and rusty jar of peanuts is considered more attractive than a pristine, beautifully-crafted dish of freshly-prepared food. Even though the attractive dish appeals to the senses and tastebuds of human beings, the bland jar appeals to one's mind and soul. The concept of *wabi* and *sabi* led to an overall change of Japan's artistic sensibility and culture overtime.

For East Asian people, Zen plays a major role in helping individuals and families express love and respect for their ancestors. Especially those cultures where the deceased relatives are believed to be in the afterlife, awaiting rebirth. The Japanese people, for instance, have small altars in their homes with the photographs of the departed, along with flowers, food, and candles. Japanese folk from all over the world head home for a festival called Obon, in August. This is called the 'Festival of the Dead'. It is believed that the dearly departed are said to return from the spirit world for one day. As morbid as it sounds, Obon is anything but. This is a time for celebration and gathering as, according to Buddha, everyone achieves enlightenment.

The Practices and Methods of Zen Buddhism

The most fascinating thing about Zen Buddhism is that it is quite paradoxical. You might be wondering why that is, even though you already have the answer at the back of your mind. Zen always requires utmost discipline of body, mind, and soul. But when it is practiced the way it's meant to be practiced, it gives one total freedom. Although one must remember that having total freedom does not mean acting impulsively. In fact, Buddhism helps you control your impulses by giving you control over them. But in order to do that, first must learn to discipline yourself. This is what makes Zen Buddhism so enigmatic.

Zen, in layman terms, is an action performed by a person. Describing the techniques and qualities of Zen is quite difficult. The only way to truly feel the essence of Zen is by practicing it. Only by practice can one fully gain an understanding of what it means to perform Zen. The major aim and goal of Zen is the perfection of one's self.

Zen meditation, known as Zazen, has always accentuated upon personal experience and that has made it a practice-oriented belief. Zazen, or the 'sitting Zen', has always been central in mediation centres. Zen instructors and monks rise early at dawn for their meditation practices which involve sitting on a cushion for long hours in total silence, without moving at all.

Zazen is mostly taught as a practice without any goals, which means there is hardly anything you have to achieve. The expression 'just sitting' is for the minds that have already reached enlightenment and awakening. In the 13th century, the forefather of the *Soto* School of

Zen, Dogen, had his own beliefs. The great founder of the esteemed school believed that the person practicing Zazen is none other than the great Buddha himself.

Zazen, in practice, is simply sitting upright with a straight posture and paying careful attention to the route of a breath in your body until you are fully active, alert, and present. Although there are several methods to perform Zazen, the aforementioned technique forms the basis of the sitting Zen.

Although life in the meditating centre revolves around sitting, Zazen is more than just mere stationary sitting. It is said that your spirit and mind extend and evolve into activities. Simple and plain activities such as eating, drinking, working, walking, are all considered as Zazen practice.

Soto Zen is considered the largest of the houses or sects of Zen in Japanese Buddhism, along with *Rinzai* and *Obaku*. Soto emphasizes greatly on meditation with no objects or contents. The practitioner practices with the goal of being fully aware and controlling the stream of thoughts flowing in and out of their mind, without interference from any foreign thoughts.

This type of Zen focuses on the concentrating on all things around one's self. An example of Soto Zen is called *Oryoki*, which involves eating meals prepared in a special ritual in the meditation hall.

Koan Meditation

Koans are paradoxical questions about reality and surroundings that cannot be answered or understood with simply the use of your conceptual mind. Students of Buddhism deal with this problem in a curriculum that has other well-known Koans as well. With the help of their mentors, the students can figure out the steps that need to be taken. According to Buddhist monks and senior teachers, the greatest Koan is how to live a fully awakened life. Koan is practiced to help students and amateurs discover non-duality without relying on their thoughts. The tradition emphasizes a great reverence for the lineage as it was influenced by the teachings of Confucius, because of the great role of monks and teachers in Zen. Koan Zen practice begins with the practitioner intensely focusing on their breath and body. They then bring up the Koan as almost a physical object with their breathing until the practitioner controls it, and lets the Koan be 'seen'. This practice is done in seclusion and is led by the monk who is teaching this marvellous meditation. The students and the teacher talk about their understanding and discuss the teachings of the Koan, which helps both parties understand it further.

Spirituality in Zen

Zen Buddhism makes us believe that we, ourselves, are the great Buddha and that Zen is the true way to discover the ultimate truth about life and spirituality. The meditation that Zen focuses upon sends one on the path to search for enlightenment within themselves. Anywhere outside one's own mind would simply be pointless, as the questions and their answers cannot originate from the same place. The truth cannot be discovered through mere rational thoughts or just secluding oneself as it takes patience of the highest level. Taking part in worship rituals and rites are common misconceptions as none of these are what Zen requires.

What is required by Zen, however, is the ultimate control of mind and body through proper meditation and mindfulness techniques. You must let go of logical thinking, as well as the questions that stem from your delusions.

Explaining the Meaning of Zen

Zen, as mentioned before, is not something that can be easily explained in words. It has no singular, universal meaning. You must have heard people associate 'being Zen' with a state of perpetual calmness. In truth, the real Zen Buddhism is not much different.

Practicing Zen means being enlightened. Not through one's personal intellect or by learning religious scriptures, but rather through the vast exploration of one's own mind. Zen is also more realistic and to-the-point. Rather than focusing on emotions or how one feels about certain things, it emphasizes more on things as they are instead of interpreting or deeply studying them. One of the most important explanations one can give about Zen is that it means to be completely alive, with your body, mind, and soul.

Bodhidharma, the great founder of Zen in China

"A special transmission outside the scriptures.
No dependency on words and letters.
Pointing directly to the human mind.
Seeing into ones in nature and attaining Buddhahood."

Zen Buddhism in North America

In the mid-20th century, Zen finally came to North America. It was introduced as a response to the violence and aggression that the early 20th century had witnessed. People began to realize that the modern culture could not save them from the great wars, such as the World Wars that took place previously. The modernist culture that the Americans had depended on wasn't helping them survive. Instead, it was the cause of large-scale suffering and pain.

A great Japanese Zen scholar by the name of Suzuki arrived to teach Zen Buddhism at the Colombia University in the early 1950s. The people who attended his lectures were greatly influenced by what the scholar had to offer. Because of his influence and success stories, other Japanese Zen monks came to settle in America within the next ten years. Newly formed Zen centres were overflowing with students who were able and eager to make solemn commitments to change their lives right away. By the late 1970s, the various traditions and teachings of Zen from the Tiger countries had been transmitted to America.

The Ultimate Aim of Zen

According to Zen beliefs, enlightenment is the inherent nature of all living beings instead of just a special quality that a handful of chosen people possess. Every soul is capable of realizing their own enlightenment simply because it is already present within. Impure thoughts such as greed, violence, and most importantly ignorance, are the root reasons why people are not aware of the power they possess. Buddhism regards these three tainted thoughts as poisons.

One of the oldest and greatest teachings of Zen is that the ordinary mind is the way to enlightenment. This ordinary mind is truly capable of understanding the nature of existence and surroundings. The practices of Zen help individuals clear their minds by analysing and emptying their minds of the previously mentioned poisons.

The ultimate aim of Zen is to offer the practitioners, whether they are students or masters, ways to restore the health of their body and soul, as well as form a connection with the creations around them. The way this is practiced has changed from culture to culture, from one region to another.

One of the greatest examples is that in medieval Japan, Zen practitioners served as healers, ministers, and even offered funeral services. In contrast, in places like Europe and parts of the West, people turned to the practice of Zen to look for inner peace and clarity of mind.

Zen, like all the other sects of Buddhism, understands that human beings suffer, and that meditation is the ultimate solution to that suffering. This meditation interconnects all human beings and helps them live a life that is aligned with the truth.

Zen Principles to Live By

The teachings of Zen are filled with practical wisdom. People far and wide have accepted the principles of Zen and embraced them to lead a much fuller and happier life. Enlightenment is not the goal of Zen teachings, but rather it is something that is gained along the way. Once you begin following certain Zen principles, you will feel your own stress and problems alleviating. You will begin to notice the peace that enters your life, and through that will you gain enlightenment.

Once you integrate these principles and ideologies into your way of life and thinking, you will find yourself reaching your goals with much ease and comfort. In the modern era, when life is lived in the fast lane and with high-intensity problems and tasks each day, we are in desperate need of some Zen help. The following Zen principles can help you lead a peaceful and stress-free life.

Happiness is Close By

Because of the competition and real-life struggles we face on the daily, we have started to think of happiness as an external element. We look towards outward sources of joy, such as a new job or a new home. We might associate happiness with moving to a different city or being with a loving partner. The truth is that if you aren't happy right now, you will not be happy even after attaining those things.

What is happiness? It is only an internal feeling that validates all your struggles and negative emotions. It helps you feel 'worth it'.

A Japanese Zen instructor by the name of Dogen once said:

"If you are unable to find the truth right where you are, where else do you expect to find it?"

The lesson we learn from this is that happiness is attainable right where you are. It is inside you, as opposed to outside somewhere in the world. Once you believe that you are happy, you will find it easier to stay happy.

The Process is What Matters

Masters of Zen and monks focus on practices, rituals, and processes rather than being fixated on the results. That is the Zen way of life. Often, we become highly obsessed with attaining a specific kind of result. This makes us forget why we started doing the thing in the first place. For example, if you are too focused on attaining perfection, with any hobby of yours, you will forget to enjoy the process. Hobbies are meant to be enjoyed, and yet in the race to become the best at it, you will have begun to inevitably hate it. It will begin to pressurize you, and you will eventually stop garnering enjoyment from this activity, leaving it behind forever.

Focus on developing habits and practices that help you support your goal, instead of the end destination. Once you focus on the process, the outcome will come to you. Don't rush the process. Follow it with determination and peace and allow it to lead you to the final stop.

Chapter 11: Zen Art

What to Know About Zen Art?

If this is your first time coming across the term 'Zen art', there are a few quick facts that you ought to know. There are two ways to discuss the concept of Zen art. The first is when you incorporate an art along with any other form of Zen activities, it is collectively known as Zen art. The second form that Zen art takes is when artists use their deep mindfulness and self-awareness and express it in their artwork. The result of this is said to be Zen art.

What Is Process Art and How to Do It?

To help you get an idea about the Process Art, let's start with something basic. The following ten steps given below show how to express process art through pouring paints.

1. Choose a wide place for work. The more space you have around you, the better. It will be quite exciting to indulge in the art. Allow yourself to be a little messy and chaotic.

In the words of the famous educator, Septima Clarke

....

"I have great belief in the fact that whenever there is chaos, it creates wonderful thinking. I consider chaos a gift."

2. Take a clean canvas of any size that you feel comfortable working with. It is preferred that you use a larger-sized canvas as that will give you a lot of space to spread your paints on it. Moreover, a bigger canvas will be easier to add more colours to than a small size canvas.

3. Bring out different containers or cups in which you can pour in significant amount of acrylic paints of different colours. Process art allows you to mix all different types of acrylic paints. Silicone oil and water-based paint options are very popular among Zen artists.

4. There are two ways to begin painting. One is to directly pour the paints on to the canvas in whatever order of colours that you like. Though this might seem like a tempting method, the alternate way of using application tools is also considerable. You don't have to use conventional artistic tools like brushes and palettes. In process art, you are encouraged to use tools that are unconventional and unorthodox, like pipes and machines.

5. Begin experimenting with the colours you are using in the painting. One by one, pour out the paint on the canvas. Allow yourself to feel every drop of it.

6. Continue with exploring and working on the paints. Finding out

what it is that makes you feel the art within yourself.

7. If you decide to play around with fire, we would advise precaution because some of the chemicals in the paints can be highly flammable. Try picking out painting options that are not dangerous if you decide to detail your art with the help of flames.

8. You can make any addition to this process that you might like. If you think merely painting on the canvas is not enough for you, you can tilt it to let the paints cover every inch. You can even split it in two, throw it on a wall, or bang it on a table. Nothing is off-limits with process art!

   In fact, instead of paints, you can also use things like charcoal, clay, mud, or syrups. Do whatever you feel would be right for your art.

9. Lastly, instead of pouring the paint out from a can, you can also use other ways to apply it on the canvas, such as using paint guns, spray bottles, or even throwing it from a distance.

The Relationship between Process Art and Zen Art

Zen art and process art have a strong relationship with each other. To best describe their connection, we must highlight the important aspects that are common in both Zen art and process art.

1. Controlling the outcomes and products of an action is impossible. Accepting this is considered crucial in both Zen Buddhism and process art. You can put in your efforts and you can practice what is in your domain, but ultimately how things end is not under your control. Your job is to agree to receive the ending.

2. Allow the process to happen on its own without interfering with it or making it more complicated. Don't add to the complexity of the method and instead try to go with the flow. Follow where the process is leading you. This, too, is important for in order to under-

stand Zen and process art.

3. Don't visualize or assume a specific kind of result during your art-work. Doing so will disrupt the whole activity and strips it of its purpose. Do art for the sake of art, not to achieve a desired result. When you dive into process art in this manner, it allows you to be free to produce art based on your individuality.

4. There is a fine line between knowing what part of the art is in your control and what is beyond it. Recognize the parts you can control and fix them accordingly. Leave what cannot be fixed and embrace the mess and imperfections that comes with it.

    Creativity is a process that doesn't need to be organised or be in a systematic form. Let it run and show itself in your art.

5. Don't judge your work. Often beginner artists have an ideal picture of an artist in their minds and try to follow their footsteps. There is no harm in that. It is a good thing to be inspired from someone else's work but try to incorporate your unique personality in your art. Try not to be too disappointed if your art doesn't look exactly like your idol's. Every artist has their own signature style, and so do you.

Insights from the Practice of Zen Art

Here are some of the meaningful insights and intuitions you can take and learn from the practice of Zen art.

- **Learning to relate**

One wonderful thing about process art is that once you learn and thoroughly grasp its concept, you can apply it to other domains of your life. This is because the knowledge and the perspective that one gains from Zen art can be applied to other areas of life to achieve a positive outcome.

This also coincides with one of the teachings of Buddhism which states that knowledge of creativity can be related to different areas in general. One thing is connected to another because knowledge is transferrable in many ways.

For example, lessons you learn in an English Literature class can be used to write a term paper on Ancient History. Political Science subjects can be used to do a presentation on Philosophy. Similarly, techniques you learn while attempting process art can be used to exhibit Zen art.

- **Connecting with nature**

Buddhism teaches us that we can't control the situation or the environment around us. However, we do have control over our actions. Buddhist teachings focus on connecting with one's surroundings.

In the words of EO Wilson:

"Nature holds the key to our aesthetic, intellectual, cognitive and even spiritual satisfaction."

The practice of Zen art allows you to process the natural elements around you and integrate them in your art, which gives it a unique kind of beauty that only you are capable of expressing.

The healing power of nature restores the balance inside your mind and soul. We are all a part of nature in one way or another. From the moment we enter this world and take our first breath, till the time of our death. We return back to nature and complete this beautiful cycle.

Going into nature is like returning back to a long-forgotten home. Using this method of process art is a form of practicing Zen Art.

- **Letting go of things**

Art is not fun if you pair it up with the anxiety and stress of controlling every stroke of brush and colors. That is what process art is teaching you, the art of letting go of the illusion of control. You're ruining all the best parts by constantly worrying about the outcome of your artwork instead of trying to enjoy the creation of something unique and possibly amazing.

Giving up on the frustrating habit of controlling everything allows you to be freer with yourself and the people around you. It is understandable that as an artist you would want your paintings and work to be top-notch, but sometimes being ambiguous about it is a wise choice. Creativity demands that you be uncertain a lot of the time.

This greatly reflects one of the teachings of Zen, which is, to let go of what you cannot control. Life was meant to be lived, not planned or controlled. Once you practice letting go of control in the process work of your art you will start looking at life from a different lens too.

- **Being spontaneous**

Another deep rooted lesson that we learn from Zen art is the essence of spontaneity. It all starts linking up in order, much like a chain. You begin by giving up the illusion of control and embracing uncertainty.

This takes you a step further into coming up with unexpected ways of mastering your art and producing spontaneous results. This wouldn't have been acquired if a certain amount of control or the pressure of being perfect was applied. In Zen art, there is a lot of space for improvisation and simply picking tricks up along the way, such as deciding what techniques, methods, or tools would work for you.

For example, you can splash the canvas with a dash of paint, use a paintbrush, or even your fingers, to complete it and see what happens in the end.

Carroll Bryant

"No matter how many plans you make or how much in control you are, life is always winging it."

That's the thing about life, right? You never know where you are going to end up even after tiresome expectations and planning. It is never guaranteed that you are going to reach your exact destination. But that shouldn't be a reason for you to start fretting right away. It is actually quite liberating to not know these things, because it saves us from a lot of exhausting tension and the worries of the future.

The divinity that has taken care of you up till now, is going to take care of things ahead as well. Relax and let go. Focus on the Zen of your life and the art for the time being.

The Many Versions of Zen Art

Once you start practicing Zen art, you will learn that there are several different ways of practicing it. Even repeating the same steps will not give you identical results, and that is just the specialty of process art. The journey is filled with surprises! There is no class or book that will teach you all there is to know about Zen Art. The wonderful unfamiliarity of not knowing everything is what makes Zen art so interesting. Simply put, this form of Buddhist art never gets boring. You always keep learning, and your state of mind keeps shifting.

Zen art teaches us that every strike of boredom can lead to something that is just waiting to be discovered. It also reminds us not to sit and plan details of our lives every single day. Low and stationary phases of life are just a reality check to step it up and head out to find or create something that nobody else has. Like Buddhist teachings, Zen art also emphasizes on the peace and calmness that is present inside of us, just waiting to be discovered.

The Originality of the Zen Art

Once you begin practicing Zen art, you will learn that every artist has their own unique style.

Every artist thrives to stick to their individuality and originality as they create their artwork. We all have their unique ideas but incorporating them into your paintings and art can get a little tough. Most artists follow common artistic techniques to bring out their inner peace on an empty canvas.

Artists who truly get involved in process art will discover how strong their power of uniqueness is. There is nobody else out there who can copy the contents of your mind.

Studying the work and paintings of others is alright as long as it is a source of inspiration and learning on the journey. If copying their style of art is done to produce the same results as them, then that is utter foolishness. Our potential for art and the way we express it differs. It is best to stick to your individuality and personality while creating art.

Doing More with Less

Like a musician who dedicates a certain amount of their time to practicing vocal exercises, every individual who plans to practice Zen art must have their own daily routine in which they practice how to visualize their art, build up a thought process, and exercise it with their personal efforts to achieve maximum results.

Do not underestimate the power of simplicity. Learn to discover ways where you gain more peace and serenity from of the art via the use of simpler materials.

Aiming for a bigger end doesn't mean you have to go equally big on the means. It is possible to attain your goal with a brevity of means.

The Zen concept of non-action works miraculously if you seriously intend to take it sincerely. Working hard and working smart are not the same things. Realize that sometimes a small fix can have bigger impact on the process art.

Zen Art Is Not Slow Art

Even though the intention behind practicing Zen art is to implement peace and patience, the process of making the artwork doesn't need to be slow or unexciting. Visual arts students, who spend a good amount of time learning minor details and dwelling on the accuracy and finer details rather than embracing ambiguity, presume that Zen art too should be like that. However, the nature of process art makes it the opposite case. Creating Zen art is about enjoying and bringing peace to yourself, nothing more.

Another important thing to have before you start making Zen art is the motivation to do so. In Buddhism, this concept is widely recognized as Bodhiccita, which is the awakening of the inner self to keep you motivated in the engagement of joyful efforts and practices. Using this mentality with the artwork keeps reminding you to move in the right direction with a proper pace.

Descartes once said: "I think, therefore I'm."

Whichever way of creating Zen art you choose to call your own, ultimately it will be a mirror reflection of your own intellectuality and individuality. One of the purposes of creating art should be to make the audience get a glimpse of what it is like inside the mind of the artist who worked on the masterpiece. The emotions, thoughts, and state of mind of the artist, is supposed to be expressed through their Zen art.

The real value of Zen art is in how you feel before, during, and after its creation. If you embody the philosophies of Zen Buddhism and incorporate them in the creation of your art, you will find your come to tranquillity and serenity.

Chapter 12: Buddhist Poetry

Buddhist poetry is a genre of literature that expands upon the Buddhist discourse. Buddhist poetry, like Buddhist art and paintings, is said to be hauntingly beautiful. Buddhist poems are meant to conjure feelings to melancholy and solitude within oneself. They reflect the aesthetic values of wabi-sabi, which refers to an emotive response to an artistic form of minimalism and solitude. Japanese Buddhist poetry covers a wide spectrum of emotions.

If we focus on the expressions and learnings of Buddhist poetry, we will find ourselves contemplating about their meaning for hours on end. To explore their message and beauty is a journey that every person who comes across Buddhist poetry undertakes.

One of the most famous Japanese poets who incorporated Buddhist learnings into their work is the well-known poet, Matsuo Basho. Matsuo Basho wrote several renowned haikus, which are poems that have three lines that feature five, seven, and five syllables. One famous poem by this poet is as follows:

furuiki ya

kawazu tobikomu

mizu no oto

This translates to:

The old pond

A frog leaps in

The sound of the water

This poem uses nature to symbolize how one moment can encompass the entire universe. This is known as the moment of awakening. It consists of the entire cosmos. This poetry combines the simplicity and nature to illustrate and portray the Buddhist theory of momentariness, which claims that chana sanshi and yinian sanqian, or "three worlds are in one moment" and "three thousand worlds are in a single thought". These phrases are contemplated upon because of their mystical nature.

There is also a certain kind of transience and impermanence portrayed in the poetry of Buddhist monks of Japan. They focus on the temporary nature of reality and the melancholy caused by its awareness and experience. An itinerant poet-artist, Saigyo Hoshi, in the late Heian period, elaborated upon the melancholic concept of experience impermanence. In his poetry, he wrote:

kokoro naki

mi ni mo aware wa

shirarekeri

shigi tatsu sawa no

aki no yugure

Its translation is as follows:

Even a body without a heart

Can still know

What melancholy is

When a snipe flies out on a marsh

In autumn twilight

Another Buddhist Zen master in the Edo period, Ryokan Taigu, alongside accepting the reality of transience and the melancholy associated with it, wrote about his failing health and old age. He mentioned the insomnia that he experienced and struggling with light and heat in the midst of darkness and cold. One of his poems is:

Old and withered I wake easily from my dreams

And find myself in an empty hall

Where there is but one candle

Struggling to persist in the long winter nights

Some say that these poems are reminders of the Mahayana insights, which state that samsara and nirvana are inseparable. Zen teachings tell us that the mind is the Buddha. Poets like Dogen identify the nature of

Buddha as impermanent, just like our minds. Our thoughts are fleeting and our minds transient. Perhaps Buddhist poetry contains elements of transience and impermanence because of this very reason.

Buddhist poetry has influence all around the world. It is not just written in Sanskrit and Japanese, but has flourished in every language that Buddhists can speak. Some other languages that Buddhist poetry has been transcribed in include Pali, Chinese, and Korean.

In the modern world, many Buddhist poets have experimented with European styles of poetry. Many of them have included values of Buddhism in undertones in their poetic compositions. Famous Buddhist poet, Miyazawa Kenji, borrows certain themes from the Lotus Sutra and integrates them in his poems. Another well-known Buddhist poem is known as the Iroha, and contains every kana in its verses. This poem is taught in Japanese primary schools for this reason. Sanskrit Buddhist poets compose in a more lyrical style.

Chapter 13: Life-Changing Buddhist Habits to Adopt

You must have noticed in pictures and videos explaining Buddhism how Buddhists always seem to look calm and peaceful. They are always so unwavering in the face of danger and disturbance, standing tall and unperturbed. You might wonder what their secret is. Do Buddhists know the key to life? Have they unlocked some deeply-buried answer to the questions and mysteries of the world? The short answer is, yes and no.

Buddhists are certainly aware of ancient philosophies and principles that make living this life much easier and comfortable. But don't worry! These hidden secrets can be unlocked by all. Even you can achieve ultimate calmness and peace. All you have to do is follow certain life-changing Buddhist habits that will completely alter your response to the challenges of life. These may appear to be difficult to implement at first, but once you adopt them you will notice an incredibly positive change in your life and they will benefit you for a lifetime.

1. Outer decluttering

Not many people know that Buddha was originally born a prince. He had the entire world at his footsteps and his every wish could have been fulfilled. Instead, he realized that the nature of materialism and desire is frustrating and shallow. Today, Buddhist monks do much of the same. They keep only a few material possessions and hold on only to the few things they need to live their life. All of these can fit in a small backpack. Just like them, decluttering your physical possessions can have a ton of positive benefits for your life.

Christina Scalise

"Clutter is the physical manifestation of unmade decisions fuelled by procrastination."

2. Inner decluttering

Inner decluttering refers to cleaning up your negative emotions and replacing them with positive ones, filled with hope and comfort. People who follow Buddhism tend to do things with the intention of doing them for the whole world and not just for themselves. Even while meditating, their intention is to attain enlightenment and power so they can help the people of the world who are suffering and in need of assistance.

Dalai Lama

"Do not let the behaviour of others destroy your inner peace."

Once you develop this kind of altruistic and selfless attitude, it is much easier to not focus on your personal problems. This makes inner decluttering much easier and simpler. You worry less about your future, dwell less on the past, and do not get as angry about unfair and unjust situations. Your mental state becomes much calmer than before. Self-ishness is truly the root of all problems.

3. Meditating

The 14th Dalai Lama

"One of the things that meditation teaches us, when we slowly descend into ourselves, is that the sense of peace already exists in us."

His book talks about meditation a whole lot. This is because this practice is central to Buddhist traditions and philosophies. The main reasons monks adopt their lifestyle is to have more time to meditate. It is said that meditation can unlock the powers of your brain that stay locked even after years of surviving in this world. A good habit is to take a few minutes out of your day every day and train your mind to be more peaceful by meditating. Meditation is believed to change your brain. You don't have to start with rigorous meditation techniques; you can always start with ten-minute yoga schedules. More on this in the later chapters.

4. **Following wise people**

Anthony J. D'Angelo

"Develop a passion for learning. If you do, you will never cease to grow."

Us humans like to believe that time is running out as we grow old. This is why we like to cram every important part of our life in our early years. Buddhism teaches us to make peace with growing old. It instructs us to attain a healthy relationship with old age. As we grow, we become wiser and gain much more spiritual knowledge than we had before. Buddhism tells us to follow wise people and to learn from them. We need to listen to their insights and words of wisdom. They have much more experience than us, and can therefore tell us a whole lot about the world that we are yet unaware of.

5. **Mindful listening**

Italian Proverb

"From listening comes wisdom, and from speaking repentance."

Buddhism focuses on using communication to help others. We must be mindful while listening to our fellow humans. This helps us understand them and ease their suffering, as well as our own. Today, listening is often constituted with being judgemental and harsh. Our minds jump to judge the next person and this is in no way helpful to us or them.

Mindful and active listening allows us to be free of judgement and critique. The aim of mindful communication is to digest what someone is saying without evaluating it. This leads to mutual respect and understanding, as well as allowing us to progress the conversation without any problems.

6. Accepting change

Robin Sharma

....

"Change is hard at first, messy in the middle and gorgeous at the end."

Buddhist master Suzuki has a crucial principle that states that change is something we all need to accept. He states:

"Without accepting the fact that everything changes, we cannot find perfect composure. But unfortunately, although it is true, it is difficult for us to accept it. Because we cannot accept the truth of transiency, we suffer."

It is a fundamental law of the universe that everything experiences change. We all change. And yet, we find it incredibly difficult to embrace. It is much easier to identify to the set precedents of this world and ourselves. We resonate with our fixed appearance, with our mind, body, and personality. When any of these changes, we suffer.

Buddhist master Suzuki reckons that we can overcome our discomfort by realizing and acknowledging that the contents of our mind are in eternal flux. Our consciousness is fleeting; it comes and goes. Once you realize this, even if you are in the heat of the moment, you will feel your anger, despair, and sorrow dissipate. In that moment, it is easy to see anger as just a moment. It comes and goes. This is why Zen teachings state that a moment is all that exists. Another one of Suzuki's quotes state:

"Whatever you do, it should be an expression of the same deep activity. We should appreciate what we are doing. There is no preparation for something else."

7. Living in the now

Buddha

"The secret of health for both mind and body is not to mourn for the past, worry about the future, or anticipate troubles, but to live in the present moment wisely and earnestly."

Buddhism urges us to embrace the present and live in every moment. As humans, that can be quite tough. We tend to worry about past events or dwell on the anxieties of the future. Our minds drift towards the fear of the unknown.

But adopting Buddhist habits means you refocus on the present. Practicing mindfulness techniques will allow you to get better at living in the moment and redirecting your thoughts to the current surroundings. With Buddhism, you are better equipped to dealing with your present engagements. Instead of harshly criticizing ourselves for getting distracted, we should simply accept that we are humans and therefore make mistakes like losing our attention.

Buddhism instructs people to, during meditation, come back to your breathing when you realize that you have lost focus. You can do this in any other situation. Focusing on the present is an incredible habit that everyone should adopt. It takes discipline, but once you have mastered it you will experience all the miracles of life.

8. Focusing on one thing at a time

Focusing on one thing might seem like a simple aspect, but it is certainly a significant one. In fact, it is a key value of Buddhist philoso-phy. Monks are taught, from the beginning, to focus on one thing at a time. They are taught to give the present their full, undivided attention. While multitasking, we feel like we accomplish a lot. But if you ever stop and notice, you will observe that you will do all the tasks you at-tempted to do at once rather poorly. Science has proven that our brains are not designed to multi-task. The quality of your work falls when you multitask.

Og Mandino

"It is those who concentrate on but one thing at a time who advance in this world."

Just like Buddhist monks, if you focus on one thing at once, you might find yourself enjoying it more and providing a better quality. You will also experience great peace and calmness.

9. **Giving your all**

Steve Maraboli

"Do the best you can, with what you can, while you can, and success in inevitable."

Giving your all means embracing everything you are doing with your whole being. This doesn't mean stressing about it or working yourself until burnout, but instead place emphasis on the current moment with peacefulness and concentration. You are in the moment and there is nowhere else you can be. Give in your all to the task at hand and wait to reap the rewards.

10. Letting go of things you cannot control

C. JoyBell C.

....

"You will find that it is necessary to let things go; simply for the reason
that they are heavy. So let them go, let go of them.
I tie no weights to my ankles."

Letting go of things is a huge part of Buddhist learnings. Buddhist monks live their entire lives letting go of things they can't control. Once you become aware of the impermanence of things, you learn to let them go and enjoy life for what it is. The best way to live life is to let go of things instead of getting attached and trying to hold on to them. Everything is susceptible to change and if you try to keep them fixed and in one place, you are resisting the natural process of things.

Questions and Answers Section

No matter how long you have been studying Buddhism, you must have some questions related to this subject. Below, we have compiled a list of FAQs (Frequently Asked Questions) that will help ease your mind and provide solutions to your problems.

Q1. Is Buddhism a religion or philosophy?

A. Well, the answer is both. Buddhism is a religion because like all other religions, it has monastics, temples, sacred texts, rituals, congregations and so forth. However, the foundation of all the religions is based on a God or Creator. In this context, there is a contradiction because Buddhism doesn't believe in any God. Therefore, sometimes, it is labelled as a philosophy, way of life or science of mind. The best term to describe Buddhism is "applied religious philosophy."

Q2. Is yoga Buddhist?

A. Yoga and Buddhism may look similar on a surface level because they share some common values. However, the two philosophies belong to different origins. Buddhism belongs to the Nastik branch of Indian philosophies. Nastik means those who don't believe in the existence of Atman or the Self. The Nastik philosophies include Buddhism and Charvak. Buddha denied the existence of a permanent self or soul. This doctrine is called "Anatta" in Pali, which is "Anatamn" in Sanskrit. Anatta translates as Non-Self.

B. On the contrary, the entire Yoga philosophy is based on the existence of Atman. The Atman is called Purusha (consciousness) in yoga philosophy. Purusha is the foundation and ultimate goal of all yoga practices. In samadhi, you become one with Purusha. Therefore, Yoga and Buddhism are absolutely opposite philosophies, though the practice of meditation is common in both.

Q3. Are there various kinds of Buddhist meditation?

A. There are different exercises taught by teachers of different Buddhist traditions and schools. Many of these exercises can only be administered by experienced meditation teachers. For the average person, however, whose aim is to realise the teachings of the Buddha, meditation is a simple process of awareness and investigation.

Q4. Is it necessary to empty your mind from thought during meditation?

A. I have cleared this concept in the chapters that emptying your mind of thoughts is a false idea and meditation has nothing to do with it. Meditation is all about focusing your attention on the present moment and becoming aware of all your thoughts and emotions without being judgemental.

Q5. I can't concentrate during meditation. Is meditation not right for me?

A. It takes time to get the hang of meditation. Therefore, if you can't concentrate, you don't need to worry. Just keep practising and whenever you feel you can't focus, take a deep breath. With time and regular practice, you will improve.

Meditation is right for anyone who wants to gain control of their thoughts, rather than their thoughts controlling them. Being mindful can help you take a mental step back from the negative thoughts that can clutter your mind, lower your self-esteem or affect your relationships. As I say that meditation or mindfulness is not magic, so It won't make your problems go away. Instead, but it will give you the ability to deal with them with a focused and relaxed mind.

Q6. How long will it take for me to become mindful?

A. To be honest, there is no standard timeframe. We all are unique and products of different life experiences. For some people, it will take a month; for others, it can take a year as well. The key is to practise with determination and persistence.

Thich Nhat Hanh, a Vietnamese Buddhist said,

"Every day we do things, we are things that have to do with peace. If we are aware of our life, our way of looking at things, we will know how to make peace right at the moment, we are alive."

Q7. What is the difference between mindfulness and relaxation?

A. Mindfulness has many benefits, and relaxation is one of them. However, relaxation is not the core purpose of mindfulness. When we talk about relaxation only, our aim is to become relaxed, and you can achieve it through anything that you enjoy. For example, you can get relaxed by watching a movie, having your favourite food, talking to a friend or just by taking a hot shower. On the contrary, the primary purpose of mindfulness is to become aware of your thoughts and surroundings without being judgemental. To achieve this purpose, you have to focus on your thoughts, body sensations, emotions or anything you are doing in the present moment. So, we can infer that the main difference between the two things is your intention.

Q8. Is there a proper way to breathe when speaking about mindfulness?

A. Mindfulness training is not about changing anything, including your breathing. The breath sensations can be used to train your mind, but you need only pay attention to the sensations you feel as the breath enters and leaves your body. So, no need to change anything. Just breathe how you normally do.

Q9. Can agnostics and atheists be Buddhist?

A. Yes, because the atheist is just someone who doesn't follow a theistic religion and doesn't believe in a god. The definition of theism is the belief in the existence of a god or gods, specifically of a creator who intervenes in the universe. The eight-fold path is not a god, nor are the forces of nature. The four noble truths are not a god, so we could say that Buddhists can be atheists.

Q10. Should I keep my eyes closed while meditating?

A. In certain schools of Buddhism it is considered acceptable to meditate and ponder with your eyes open. Others instruct you to close your eyes. In case you choose to keep your eyes open, where you choose to look depends on the kind of meditation you are performing. Usually, you are instructed to look down and shorten your gaze while meditating in order to calm and concentrate your mind. Once you lift your eyes, widen your gaze and allow the environment to sink in.

The good way to meditate is to lower your gaze six feet in front of you and keep it focused and relaxed. Your gaze should not be too tight or too loose. Your eyes help you battle obstacles while meditating. When your mind is overactive, keep your gaze short and low. When your mind is numb, raise your eyes and take in more of the world around you.

Q11. What do the following Buddhist terms mean: vipassana, zazan, vipashyana, shamatha, calm-abiding, insight, and mindfulness?

A. There are different ways that different schools of Buddhism approach meditation. However, concentration and insight are what unites all of Buddhism's meditations. Mindfulness and self-awareness are some of the names used to define these practices. Buddhist meditations start with relaxing and then concentrating your mind by following your breathing. They are started this way because an unstable and fear-centred mind is in no position to develop any insight. There is no way that you can, with a mind like that, take a step into the nature of reality.

Practicing techniques that awaken your insight is strictly a Buddhist speciality. When your mind is stable and fully focused, you can explore the depth and nature of reality with ease. It is ideal to not contemplate on what you might discover and just enjoy the concepts and ideas that form in your mind. This personal journey can certainly be quite eye-opening. Good luck with yours!

Q12. Do Buddhists take any vows? Which ones do they take and why?

A. Just like most religions around the globe, Buddhism requires you to take some vows too. There are several different kinds of vows to be taken, some detailed and others minimal. Most of them address an individual's intentions and ethics. Some monastics vow to follow certain rules that govern their daily lifestyles, such as vowing to remain celibate. Others, like Lay Buddhists, vow to stay true to the five main precepts which consist of no lying, stealing, killing, sexual misconduct, and intoxicants.

Some people say that you attain formal status as a Buddhist by taking a vow called the Refuge Vow. This means acknowledging that there is no freedom from suffering and that one can only take refuge in Buddha, dharma, and sangha. Additionally, Buddhists take the bodhisattva vow, in which they vow to forego their enlightenment until all beings in the world are freed from suffering. Certain Buddhist school followers take the basic vow, which is to see everything around you as sacred and enlightened. All beings are Buddhas and all sounds are mantras. The outer world is said to be a mandala.

In Buddhism, vows are like compasses. They are simply a way to stay on the correct path. You may be unaware of your destination or if you will ever reach it, but your vows point to the right direction. This is the direction you must keep moving in. living in this vow is said to be the path itself.

Q13. Is it normal for my breathing to feel uncomfortable during meditation?

A. There is no wrong way to breathe during meditation. Buddhist meditation, unlike yoga, does not require you to breathe a certain way. While practicing mindfulness, our breathing is focused upon, but you shouldn't try to control it. You should simply become aware of it, without trying to change it. In fact, the reason that you might be experiencing discomfort is because you are trying to control your breathing in some small way. The best way to achieve peak serenity during Buddhist meditations is to let go of trying. Allow yourself to be free. Doing a small routine of yoga can help pace your breathing before meditation. Take slow and deep breaths in order to reflect and become aware.

Q14. What is the definition of a sin in Buddhism?

A. Commonly, a sin is a moral or religious violation. The Buddha was not God, and hence did not hand down any commandments or religious code of conducts. If you don't obey his teachings, you are not eternally damned, like with religions. Elaborating upon that, the issue of good vs. evil is not the main ideology that Buddhism revolves around. The central theme of Buddhism is ignorance vs. wisdom. Buddhists believe that we do not fully comprehend the nature of ourselves and the world around us. Buddha's second noble truth is that the real cause of suffering is lack of knowledge, or ignorance. Ignorance is what creates the toxicities that are attachment, aggression, and anger. Good vs. evil is not our first mission. It is to attain knowledge and awareness.

Of course, adopting moral and ethical values hold extreme importance to the Buddhist world. And yet, even more crucial is to change our nature from harmful to open and interdependent. We must accept that we are ever-changing.

Q15. What is Kadampa Buddhism?

A. Kadampa Buddhism is a school of Mahayana Buddhism founded by a famed Indian Buddhism teacher, Master Atisha. First known in Tibet, this branch of Buddhism grew in that region for over hundreds of years before spreading out into the world. Today, there are 800 Kadampa centres around the globe. Each centre has its own of society and language, where they practice Kadampa Buddhism. Kadampa Buddhism follows the path of enlightenment as set by Buddha. This is based on Buddha's special presentation known as 'Lamrim'. Kadampa Buddhism focuses on accessibility and ensures that people from all walks of life can easily understand and practice this form of Buddhism.

Q16. Should I stop going to therapy now that I have started Buddhist meditation?

A. Buddhist purists do believe that the wisdom and compassion we formulate from meditation practices is all we need as this targets our sufferings and tries to ease them effectively.

Western Buddhist practitioners on the other hand, insist that meditation works best when paired up with Western psychology. The best way to leave behind your worries and anxieties and free yourself from trauma and negative emotions is to combine psychotherapy and meditation. Buddhist meditation unveils our thoughts and emotions, whereas Western psychology deals with their contents and aftermath. Today, many Buddhist teachers are also psychotherapists. Whether you want to choose therapy, meditation, or both, you are in good hands.

Q17. Why does Buddhism revolve around suffering?

A. The translation of the first noble truth is that "Life is marked by suffering". Suffering is something we may not always experience, but it always present. Even when we have joy and happiness, we cannot escape from the clutches of suffering. The suffering of not achieving what we desire and the suffering of losing it when we do get it. An underlying suffering and anxiety is constantly a part of us.

The word dukkha, used to represent suffering, actually means a wheel that isn't smooth and round, but bumpy. It can only allow for a bumpy ride. That is what life is. It is nothing but an unending series of mistakes. Buddhism doesn't focus on suffering and beings tuck in it, instead it focuses on letting go of that suffering. Buddhist teaches state that one becomes much happier and freer once he lets go of his suffering. Suffering is said to be a cause of hope, not of sorrow. It is the first step to enlightenment.

Q18. What differentiates a Buddhist church from a Buddhist temple and a Buddhist centre?

A. The difference between these three depends on the specific school of Buddhism. When Japanese immigrants arrived in the United States of America, they set up temples to practice Shin Buddhism in. Shin Buddhism is a popular Japanese Buddhism sect. As time went on, they established Buddhist Churches in America to gain acceptance in the American society. These churches are similar in physical and hierarchical structure to Christian churches.

Chinese and South Asian Buddhists prefer to use the world 'temple' instead of church. These temples have a united community and a pastoral aspect. Members of the Buddhist temples observe celebrations and rely on them for the rites of passage, like weddings and funerals.

Buddhist centres were created by Western Buddhist practitioners who created them to offer programs and retreats where Buddhism is practiced and taught.

Q19. I get drowsy or sleepy during meditation. Is that normal?

A. The truth is, as long as meditation has been around, its practitioners have had to combat drowsiness and sleepiness! This shouldn't come as a surprise. We go through highs and lows of energy throughout our day– why shouldn't we during meditation?

Drowsiness, sleepiness, and agitation, are just a few of the obstacles that one encounters during meditation. Some antidotes include straightening your posture and raising your gaze. Allow yourself to see more space and light around you. When your mind is agitated, lower your gaze and make it shorter. Concentrate on a specific area and on your breath.

In any case, you do not have to condemn yourself for feeling sleepy or frustrated during meditation. Some effort is required to ground yourself. Listen to the signals your body is sending you. Perhaps you need more sleep, or maybe you are hungry. Maybe you are trying not to dwell on a particular incident that is bringing negative emotions into your meditation hours. Either way, use your body's reactions as a sign and a reminder to return to your breathing and meditation.

Q20. What is the bump that is depicted on top of Buddha's head in paintings and statues?

A. In general, historical statues of Buddha are intended to represent the spirit of Buddha and his realization and attainment. These qualities are to be sought after and aspired to achieve. These often include spiritual symbols like halos and other signs.

The bump on top of Buddha's head is the ushnisha or the turban. It is one of the thirty-two marks of Buddha's physical body. The turban appears as round or conical in most paintings. It may also be pointed or flame-like. When shaped like a flame, the ushnisha is meant to symbolize spiritual power. Some followers see it as a crown, conveying the royalty and supreme control of Buddha's enlightenment. The historic and original Buddha, however, had a normal human head.

Notes

(1) Encyclopedia. (2020). Buddhism, History of Science and Religion. Retrieved from: https://www.encyclopedia.com/education/encyclopedias-almanacs-transcripts-and-maps/buddhism-history-science-and-religion

(2) Encyclopedia. (2020). Buddhism, History of Science and Religion. Retrieved from: https://www.encyclopedia.com/education/encyclopedias-almanacs-transcripts-and-maps/buddhism-history-science-and-religion

(3) Encyclopedia. (2020). Buddhism, History of Science and Religion. Retrieved from: https://www.encyclopedia.com/education/encyclopedias-almanacs-transcripts-and-maps/buddhism-history-science-and-religion

(4) Encyclopedia. (2020). Buddhism, History of Science and Religion. Retrieved from: https://www.encyclopedia.com/education/encyclopedias-almanacs-transcripts-and-maps/buddhism-history-science-and-religion

(5) Encyclopedia. (2020). Buddhism, History of Science and Religion. Retrieved from: https://www.encyclopedia.com/education/encyclopedias-almanacs-transcripts-and-maps/buddhism-history-science-and-religion

(6) Encyclopedia. (2020). Buddhism, History of Science and Religion. Retrieved from: https://www.encyclopedia.com/education/encyclopedias-almanacs-transcripts-and-maps/buddhism-history-science-and-religion

(7) Saisuta, P. (2012). The Buddhist Core Values and Perspectives for Protection Challenges: Faith and Protection. Retrieved from: https://www.unhcr.org/50be10cb9.pdf

(8) Saisuta, P. (2012). The Buddhist Core Values and Perspectives for Protection Challenges: Faith and Protection. Retrieved from: https://www.unhcr.org/50be10cb9.pdf

(9) Saisuta, P. (2012). The Buddhist Core Values and Perspectives for Protection Challenges: Faith and Protection. Retrieved from: https://www.unhcr.org/50be10cb9.pdf

(10) Castro, J. (2013). What is Karma? Live Science. Retrieve from: https://www.livescience.com/41462-what-is-karma.html

(11) Lumen. (2020). Buddhism Today. Website. Retrieved from: https://courses.lumenlearning.com/atd-fscj-worldreligions/chapter/buddhism-today/#:~:text=In%20the%2021%20century%20CE,Japan%2C%20Korea%2C%20and%20Vietnam.

(12) Arrowiver. (2020). The Four Foundations of Mindfulness. Website. Retrieved

from: https://www.arrowriver.ca/dhamma/founMind.html

(13) Arrowiver. (2020). The Four Foundations of Mindfulness. Website. Retrieved from: https://www.arrowriver.ca/dhamma/founMind.html

(14) Arrowiver. (2020). The Four Foundations of Mindfulness. Website. Retrieved from: https://www.arrowriver.ca/dhamma/founMind.html

(15) Arrowiver. (2020). The Four Foundations of Mindfulness. Website. Retrieved from: https://www.arrowriver.ca/dhamma/founMind.html

(16) Mindful. (2020). Getting Started with Mindfulness. Website. Retrieved from: https://www.mindful.org/meditation/mindfulness-getting-started/

Thank you.

Thank you very much for taking the time to read this book. I hope it positively impacts your life in ways you can't even imagine.

If you have a minute to spare, I would really appreciate a few worlds on the site where you bought it. Honest feedbacks help readers find the right book for their needs!

Dharma Amanthi

Made in United States
North Haven, CT
21 March 2022

17385602R00065